LORAL COUNTY TIMES:

Return to Echo Woods

LUCKY MAXWILL

BALBOA.
PRESS
A DIVISION OF HAY HOUSE

Balboa Press books may be ordered through booksellers or by contacting:

Balboa Press
A Division of Hay House
1663 Liberty Drive
Bloomington, IN 47403
www.balboapress.com
1 (877) 407-4847

Print information available on the last page.

ISBN: 978-1-5043-8758-3 (sc)
ISBN: 978-1-5043-8760-6 (hc)
ISBN: 978-1-5043-8759-0 (e)

Library of Congress Control Number: 2017914045

Balboa Press rev. date: 11/17/2017

DEDICATION

This book is presented in memory of Jake and Lucy Hammontree, William and Maxine Byler and Loral Craig Byler. Their stories entertained me as a child and fostered an adult who is a perpetual daydreamer that loves books and writing.

I dedicate this tale to my daughter (Jill), son (Joe), son-in-law (Steve) and three extraordinary grandchildren (Kylie, Trevor and Katelyn).

ACKNOWLEDGMENT

I am forever grateful to friends, educators and family members who provided generous moral support as I wrote this tale about animals and an idyllic Missouri.

Special thanks go to art director and artist, Dr. Barbara Peck, and artist David Diekamp. They created visual representations of locations, main characters, special animals and Civil War artifacts.

As an advocate of educators who are the gold standard of patience and guidance for all future generations, I want to thank those who contributed their insight and gave me their undivided attention and input. Alphabetically those include: Mary Margaret Campbell Brown, Tina Kephart Garrison, Marilyn Riley Mongan, Dr. Barbara Peck and Ann Seymour.

Unbiased, honest and critical input was also provided by a select group of junior readers. However, due to their age they shall remain anonymous. But, the little darlings know who they are.

This book would not be possible without the encouragement I received from family members, and dear friends who I consider my extended family. Alphabetically they are: Carlee Cellar, Sue Gale, Jona Lynch Gordon (cousin), Joy Ann Koski-Holm, Gloria Joyce Lynch (cousin), Carla Talent-McManus, Dr. Barbara Peck, Rev. Cecilia Rodarte, Sharon (Kay) Walker and Diane Wilhite (sister).

And finally, my journey in a career as a writer was heavily influenced by the inspirational teachings of the Rev. Dr. Jane Claypool, Carolyn Sheila Baxter and Rev. Cecilia Rodarte, as well as the educational guidance by University of Nevada–Las Vegas, (UNLV) journalism professor Dr. Barbara Cloud.

CHAPTER 1

IT WAS A MUGGY SPRING morning and sharp patterns of lightning zigzagged across the cloudy country sky. Squirrels chattered and crows squawked, alerting creatures within a country mile that a storm was brewing, would hit at 12:33 p.m. and last for 37 minutes. A light breeze swept through the long open windows of Audry Merryweather's kitchen and brushed gauzy curtains softly against the freshly scrubbed wooden window frames.

She had awakened early that morning and made a shopping list for her trip to Springfield the next day. She needed to buy new hardware for the old cupboards, paint, new lamp shades, and a cabinet for her music system.

Audry was looking forward to redecorating the old family homestead where she now lived. She had moved in only a couple of months ago, right after her 21st birthday. The place held the best of Audry's childhood memories, and she was devoted to returning it to its original charm and presence in Echo Woods.

As she sat eating her breakfast of biscuits, jam, and creamed sassafras tea, a sudden gust of wind blew open the heavy, creaking kitchen door that led outside. Then, the screen door loudly slammed behind it.

Unannounced, and quick as a flash, a small person, barely taller than the kitchen counter, slipped into the room.

Audry gasped, too frightened to speak or move.

"Hi-ho, don't mind me. I'll just put my things over here, and we can visit," the self-assured intruder said in a lilting voice as he slipped past the kitchen table.

After the shock wore off, Audry jumped up and yelled, "Excuse me! Who *are* you?!"

Without hesitating, the uninvited visitor calmly replied, "Well, it doesn't really matter now. We'll get acquainted soon enough. But, since you asked, my name is Sutherland Angus MacGregor. I was named after my great-great grandfather Sutherland Angus MacGregor, the first. To some I am Mac, but most of my friends call me Sam. That's short for my full given name. Yes, I know—it's a lot to think about. But, my dear mother thought it would be best for my promoters to give me a proper business name once I became better known for my talents. For now, though, you can call me by my mother's favorite name for me—Sam. She said I reminded her of a charismatic mayor she knew once upon a time by the same name. He also was—"

Immediately, Audry interrupted his rambling introduction. "Talents?" she asked. "Sutherland Angus Macgregor ... **Sam**??!" With each question, her voice grew louder, until she stamped her foot and asked, "What **are** you talking about?!!"

BAM!!! A brilliant flash of lightning lit up the kitchen, followed by a crack of thunder that split the sound barrier and silenced the entire county for three seconds.

The house shook, the kitchen windows rattled, and Audry's heart raced! Outside the trees were shaking so badly, she thought for a second they might want to run away.

Audry grabbed the edge of the kitchen counter to steady herself and stared at the strange being in front of her. She had *never* seen anybody like him before.

Looking into Audry's green eyes, Sam proudly proceeded, "Why yes, let me explain. I am a magician and piper of sorts, and I do many kinds of odd and sometimes strange jobs. A friend of mine at the sheriff's office thought maybe I could help you out, since you haven't lived here very long. I have had many successes in my time in this line of work and have even tamed shrews, werewolves, wild hares and mules, as well as some elements of Mother Nature.

"Here, let me give you my card. It's all there," he offered. And with a slight bow, Sam presented Audry with a business card. Still somewhat shaken, Audry slowly took the card and placed it next to her shopping list.

Confused and shaken, Audry wasn't sure if she was dreaming, or if she was coming down with some kind of bug. But right now, she felt a bit dizzy and slowly slid back down in her kitchen chair.

She barely knew the local population, except for maybe a couple of people that she might have met at the local market or maybe at her job at the legal aid office. And certainly she didn't know anybody with the sheriff's office. Then again, it was a small rural area, and word about newcomers traveled fast.

Audry realized immediately that she could ***never ever*** mention this encounter to anybody. She herself barely believed the conversation with Sam had actually taken place, and she was positive nobody else would.

Yet, there he was, having appeared out of nowhere—a male midget of sorts. *Little people* was the correct term, but Audry wasn't sure whether the reference applied to this person.

He looked like a mature adult but was no taller than a five-year-old child whose ears and nose were odd. A navy blue hunting cap covered his flyaway peach-colored hair. He wore khaki knickers and short buckled boots, which presumably made quick entries and exits easy for him.

He appeared to be well-fed and happy-go-lucky. His sky-blue shirt, with a number of small pockets, matched his eyes, which twinkled when he spoke.

With growing impatience, Audry stood up and exclaimed, "Mac, or Sam, whatever your name, I am not interested! There are no shrews or werewolves around here, and Mother Nature seems to have everything under control. I'm working on many projects right now, and I do not appreciate your intrusion. You can't just barge into my house. Besides, I don't know who you really are!"

Unfazed, Sam nonchalantly continued, "Well, let me assure you, my intentions are purely honorable, and I know there are many tasks needing attention around here. No disrespect, young lady, but those fences have been down for a long time, and the grain bins need to be repaired. And, although you have a grand old barn, the loft has loose boards, and the pump for the well inside is beyond repair.

The workshop, stable, and other buildings need their roofs patched, and that old greenhouse wouldn't stand up to a good puff of wind! Absolutely, new paint will put a friendly face on this fine old property. I have some great associates, who'll help me—once I get started."

"But I haven't hired you, and I am doing quite well, thank you very much!" Audrey protested as she continued to study Sam.

Sam gave a quick smile that looked more like a smirk and said, "Well, you see, my work comes as a 'public service' you might say, and it won't take me long. And trust me, you will be more than pleased." Before Audry could speak, Sam quickly slid into a chair at her kitchen table.

"But first I'll need a cup of tea to get me started. And thank *you* so much!" Sam continued.

Dumbfounded, Audry had no immediate response, but she thought he was right. She *did* need some help, but this was a lot to think about, and she wasn't sure she could trust this small "good Samaritan" who appeared out of nowhere.

Briefly she thought about grabbing Sam by the seat of his pants and throwing him out the kitchen door. But she decided that wasn't a good idea, because he seemed to be a scrappy type. Instead she moved to the stove to make him a cup of tea. She would show him the door later.

Audry set a cup of tea and saucer down on a napkin in front of Sam. Reaching past the tea, he grabbed two biscuits and the pot of jam. Smiling back at Audry he announced, "Oh, and I could use some ice water after I'm finished with work for today."

The idea that someone so small, intrusive, and rude was sitting in her kitchen, and then demanded to have ice water later, was simply too much for Audry to tolerate.

She grabbed the plate of biscuits and jam pot from the table and crossed the kitchen to store them. When she turned around, intending to tell the intruder he must be on his way, Sam was gone. Without a sound, he had disappeared, though his backpack was still sitting on the floor near the kitchen door.

All that remained on the table was his empty tea cup and some crumbs on a napkin. This was alarming. Where could he have disappeared to so quickly?

Immediately, Audry started searching the roomy old house for him. She looked in the front entry way, the stairwell to the basement, and even the basement itself.

She then searched the family library, her office, the bedrooms, and the stairs leading up to the attic. She looked in the back porch that led to the storm cellar. After a 10-minute search, Audry could not find Sam. Bewildered, Audry stepped back into the kitchen and was startled once again when she heard the screen door slam behind her.

Sam stood smiling at her and declared, "Well, I think you will find that better."

Audry was almost reluctant to hear the answer to her question, but she curtly asked it anyway. "What?" she asked. "What is better?"

"Oh, I took care of that big pile of logs. They're all split and stacked and ready for your fireplace," Sam proudly said.

Audry thought, "Not only is he rude, he's also a fibber!" And to prove her point, she marched to the window intending to show him nothing had changed.

But to her utter astonishment, the mountain of cut timber was gone, and the logs had been split and stacked neatly near the house. How had he done that, so quickly? He wasn't even dirty!

"Wh-a-at? How?" Audry stammered.

Sam looked pleased with himself and said, "Oh, no need to thank me. It was nothing. You *will* need to get a new axe, though."

Audry was speechless and a bit embarrassed. Finally she said, "Well, I have no idea who you are or how you did that so quickly. But, thank you. I don't understand how you moved those logs by yourself and split and stacked so much wood in—"

Sam interrupted, "You're welcome, but I'll need that ice water now. By the way, here is a list of supplies I'll need to get your place shaped up."

He retrieved a fistful of small sheets of paper from one of his shirt pockets. There were more than a dozen sheets, with items listed on both sides, written in strange, loopy handwriting.

Sam eagerly drank the water Audry had poured for him and started toward the door. Turning back to Audry, he advised, "You shouldn't worry so much, Miss Audry. Good will is everywhere. Sometimes it is just difficult to understand or accept. I'll be back tomorrow. But, it isn't polite to ask a whole lot of questions about charity or a gift. And, again, you're welcome!"

Then, before she could blink, he was gone.

Audry sat down at the kitchen table trying to figure out what she *thought* had happened. The events were so absurd that she was having doubts. Had she imagined it? Apparently not, because there was the clear evidence of the stacked wood outside, and inside on the table an empty tea cup and a business card. Again, she reminded herself that she certainly could not tell anybody about her visitor or the chopped wood, because *nobody* would believe her. But who, she wondered, *was* Sam?

Those ears and nose were like none she'd ever seen before! From a side view, the upper edge of his ear looked like a cartoon drawing of the top of a heart, except it sloped forward. The nose resembled something that had been sculpted from putty by a sculptor who had finished it with a short tug, creating its upturned end.

After going over every detail in her mind to try and make sense of everything, she vaguely remembered a story her grandmother had once told her. The strange events had occurred much farther down south in the state in the Ozark Mountains.

According to her grandmother, nothing really bad had happened, except there were some unexplained mysteries. Vehicles were moved to other locations in the middle of the night, the power went down and the phones quit working. Nobody knew for sure how long the phones or power was out, but everything was back to normal by sunrise the next morning.

Nothing had seemed out of the ordinary at the time except for the appearance of a group of out-of-town visitors. They had stopped at a country store to get a spare tire fixed and buy some horse liniment. The only thing unusual about these customers was the red medicine wagon they pulled behind a large, yellow truck with wooden stock racks. Not many people could recall seeing a real-life medicine wagon before, at least not in that backwoods area. After all, wagons like that mostly turned up near carnivals in larger towns, not in rural areas of the <u>Ozark Mountains</u> in Missouri.

But right before the truck left the store, the clerk noticed a couple of unusually short folks who were smoking pipes, and had scrambled to jump into the truck before it lurched back onto the road. Taking a closer look before they disappeared, he noticed their very quaint ears and noses and realized … they looked like elves.

Audry wondered if Sam could be a relative of those visitors in the hills so long ago. She thought about checking the old family library the next day to see if *maybe* there was something written down in an old diary that had been handed down. Unfortunately, somebody had moved many of the old books that used to line the shelves and she had not yet been able to locate them in the old house.

But now, Audry was exhausted from the day's events. Tomorrow she needed to finish up her "to-do" list. And that meant getting what she needed in Springfield. She only had a couple of days left before she had to get back to work on projects for the legal aid office.

At the moment, she needed sleep. With all of the abnormal events of the day, though, Audry tossed and turned, recalling all the events of the day—repeatedly. Suddenly she remembered the card Sam had given her.

"Yes!" she said aloud before drifting off to sleep. In the morning, she would put the card in her wallet for safekeeping. She had a feeling she would need it.

Audry

Sam

CHAPTER 2

AUDRY'S ENCOUNTER WITH AN ELF was indeed unbelievable. But Loral County, and especially Echo Woods, was never what it appeared to be to outsiders, at least for *some* outsiders. Its obscure location made it sometimes hard to find, even though it was a narrow and long county right in the heart of Missouri that extended north to south for over 200 miles. On a map, its outline looked most like an eagle's feather. From Echo Woods, it was a good three-day drive to the Pacific Ocean if you went to Joplin and headed west. But visitors to mid-Missouri who wanted to go to Echo Woods were directed by locals to go to Bingville, make a hard left turn at the giant live oak tree, and proceed until the Echo Woods sign appeared. All were assured, "You can't miss it."

For Audry, most of her memories of Echo Woods were associated with the home during her visits to see her grandparents, Levi and Lizzie Merryweather. Originally built in 1880 by Levi's great-great grandfather Jacob Merryweather, the house stood proud and solid. It was surrounded by pastures, timber, and a small branch of icy cold water that flowed through the property.

Audry remembered flying at the age of seven with her parents, Phil and Julie, from southern California to visit her grandparents and her dad's brother, Uncle Mike, at the homestead. Neither her dad nor Uncle Mike wanted to settle around Echo Woods once they were grown. They said it was too boring, but they enjoyed the family visits and some of the rare adventures that occurred. They had chosen much more exciting lifestyles. Her dad, a former Marine, now sought the thrills as a stuntman in Hollywood. And, Uncle Mike was a proud member of the Peace Corps in South America. He helped to build roads and find new markets for the villagers' goods. He had learned new languages and even how to cook exotic foods, including insects.

When she visited Echo Woods as a child, Audry would be greeted by her grandparents with lots of hugs and questions about her school, friends, and surfing at the beach. She really loved her grandmother's thick soft chocolate chip cookies.

Although the cookies were always a delight, she also enjoyed searching for new baby kittens in the barn with her grandfather. He would tell her the latest tales about all the animals that roamed freely on the property, where no hunting was ever allowed. It was like a wilderness preserve that deer, rabbits, foxes, raccoons, a few clumsy opossums, ground hogs, squirrels, hawks, ravens, crows, owls, Canada geese, and every imaginable bird could call "home."

The next morning, Audry overheard Grandpa Merryweather talking to her dad and Uncle Mike about a special rose garden he wanted them to help build for Grandma Merryweather. "She has wanted one for years, and I have just been too busy. How about you boys helping me?" he asked.

"Sure. What do you need us to do?" her father asked.

Uncle Mike jokingly asked, "Do I need to pack a lunch?"

"No, goofy," Grandpa responded. "I just need you to load and haul some of the old rich dirt from the persimmon grove to that spot I've staked off near the side porch. Shouldn't take you very long."

Although it sounded like a simple job, they both knew it would take some heavy shoveling and loading into a wagon pulled by the tractor.

"Okay, Dad, we're on it," Audry's dad responded. "Mike, you drive. Audry and I will ride in the wagon."

"Yes!" Audry happily responded.

Together, the three trudged to the machine shed. Audry watched as her dad and Uncle Mike hooked up the tractor to the wooden wagon and threw in some long-handled shovels. Her dad then lifted Audry up, put her in the wagon and climbed in beside her.

"Now hold on tight to the edge," he cautioned.

Slowly, Uncle Mike started the tractor, put it in gear, slipped the clutch, and jerked slowly forward. He then drove the tractor toward a small pasture hidden by scrub woods and into the persimmon grove. Once there, Uncle Mike stopped the tractor near the edge of the trees, backed the wagon toward the old grove, and cut the engine.

"Okay, now what?" Uncle Mike asked.

"Well, let's look for some old rich dirt and shovel it into the wagon. It's probably the first time it's been touched in decades," her dad replied.

They walked around together looking for an easy spot and remarked about how the old grove had grown since they were boys.

"Remember when we used to hide out in here and play war?" Uncle Mike asked her dad.

"Yeow, but, I **really** remember when we tried to eat the persimmons too early before they were ripe and how it made me want to puke!" her dad said, and pretended to gag.

"But look at it now. There are some apple trees that are starting to grow over there," Uncle Mike said as he pointed to an outside area of the grove. "Wonder how they got started here? And now there are all of those honeysuckle bushes. I don't remember those being here. It's really gotten thick, but good shelter for the wildlife."

Audry wandered around and saw that at the lower end of the hill where the grove ended, water was seeping out of the ground. "Dad, look there," she pointed out.

"Yeow, and it's cold too. Spring water." he said.

"Let's start over next to those really old trees closest to the wagon," her dad suggested.

Both men grabbed shovels and poked the ground until they found soft, black dirt that they scooped and shoveled into the wagon. After about a half hour, Uncle Mike said, "Don't you think that is plenty?"

"Well, could be," her dad replied. "Let me get a couple more scoops next to that biggest tree over there. Then that should be enough."

He went back near the largest persimmon tree and thrust the shovel head into the soft soil. Although the previous digging had been easy, her dad's shovel hit something very hard and immovable.

He slowly poked at the spot again, and again hit something solid that produced a metallic sound. He carefully scooped away small amounts of dirt to see exactly what he had hit.

"What've you got there, Phil? Monster rocks?" Uncle Mike asked.

"I don't know, but I'm about to find out," he replied. As he pushed away more dirt, a couple of inches of a metal object appeared. "What the heck?" he muttered to himself.

Excited, down on his knees, he pulled a knife from his pocket and unfolded one of its long, broad blades. Cautiously, he poked at the soil, scooping out small amounts with his hands. Gradually, more of the metal was revealed including an attached short thick chain.

Audry and Uncle Mike could not contain their curiosity and watched as Audry's dad steadily unearthed the mysterious metal mass from the grasp of the earth. Finally, with a gentle but firm tug, he pulled what looked like a very old bucket sealed with a lid, out of the ground. As he slowly raised it in the air for his brother and Audry to see, Audry could hear something faintly rattling inside.

"We need to show this to Dad," her father said with a sense of mystery. "This is really old, and nothing like I've ever seen before."

"Is it a treasure?" Audry asked with her eyes wide open.

"It could be," her dad responded with uncertainty.

CHAPTER 3

As soon as her Uncle Mike had stopped the rig back in the barn lot, Audry, jumped out and ran to the house as fast as her young legs could carry her. She excitedly threw open the back door.

"GRAND-PA!" she hollered. She ran into his office, where she found him reading some papers.

"What is it, Sunshine? What has got you all stirred up?" he asked with amusement.

"We found something!" Audry breathlessly proclaimed.

"What—a bird's nest? Or a timber rattler?" he continued to question.

"No!" she responded emphatically. "We found a treasure!"

"What?" he asked, as his face became more serious.

"Yes, Dad found it when they were digging, and he's not sure what it is! Something metal with stuff inside. I think it's important!" she exclaimed.

"Hmmm, well, let's go see what you're talking about," he said, as he got up and tried to follow Audry, who had shot out the door like a racehorse.

Outside, she caught up with her dad and Uncle Mike as they backed the wagon near the site for the new rose garden.

"Dad!" Audry shouted, "Show Grandpa what you found."

"Okay, give me a second," her dad replied. He went to a corner of the wagon and pulled the dirty, corroded bucket to show his father. Holding it with both hands, Audry's dad carefully held it chest high so that his father could see what he had uncovered.

"Oh my! Phil, I'm not really sure what you have there," Levi replied with an unusual expression of surprise and curiosity.

"I don't know either, but there is something inside," Audry's dad said as he slowly rocked the bucket from side to side. The contents moved around, creating a muffled noise.

Carefully touching its top and chain, Levi remarked, "This is very, very old, and I don't have a clue what it is. But I think my buddy in St. Louis can unseal the lid and tell us more about what this might be. He is curator of one of the best historical museums in the country. Let me take a photo with my digital camera and I'll email him."

"Julie, Audry, and I are planning on going to St. Louis to see a ballgame in a couple of days. If he's interested, we can show it to him in person," Audry's father suggested.

"Sounds good. I really want to know what you've found there," Levi said.

Within a day, Levi's friend Ray called him about the bucket. "From the picture, it looks like you've got yourself a collector's item, Levi. I think it's from the Civil War. Tell your son to come by, and I'll find out more," Ray assured Levi.

CHAPTER 4

AUDRY WAS THE MOST EXCITED about the trip to St. Louis. Yes, the ballgame would be fun, but she couldn't wait to hear what the museum director thought about the old bucket, and especially to find out what was inside.

On their way to St. Louis a couple of days later, Audry as usual was full of questions. Audry *always* asked a *lot* of questions.

After a while, she developed new interest in the scenery along the highway. The landscape was different from the desertscape of southern California. Everything was so green and the fields of crops were endless. She saw herds of cattle, goats and lambs as well as a lot of wildlife. Occasionally she caught glimpses of deer as they bounded into thick wooded areas near creeks.

"Audry, soon you'll see the big Mississippi River when we get to St. Louis," her mother said. "I have an old friend who actually operates a tugboat that pushes barges up and down the river," she explained.

"Barges? What are those?" Audry asked.

"They are large, flat-bottomed boats that are loaded with grain, equipment, or other products, and the tugboats transport them to docks or landings along the river where they can be unloaded," her mother explained. "Tugs are like tractors on the river, and barges are like wagons. There are even barges designed for special events called party barges," she continued.

"We might also see the large art museum near the zoo," her mother explained. She was particularly interested in the museum because she was an art teacher. As a teenager living in Missouri, she had enjoyed painting and drawing birds in the parks, as well as wildlife she saw along the Missouri and Mississippi Rivers.

Once they arrived at the historical museum, the receptionist told Audry's dad that the curator was expecting him and would be out as soon as his meeting ended. Her dad had carried the bucket in a wooden box covered with an old blanket, and placed it next to the receptionist's station.

While they waited, Audry became fascinated with all of the displays and photos that provided a glimpse into Missouri's past history. She learned that, originally Missouri was part of the Louisiana Purchase that took place in 1803, and that it became a state in 1821.

Her dad told her how her grandfather's great-great grandfather, Jacob Merryweather, had played a role in Missouri's history as well.

He told her that Jacob had worked as a surveyor. He had traveled all around Loral County surveying land that marked property lines for sections of land. Section hands helped to lay railroad tracks for the trains, or "iron horses," that were making their way west. The train was part of the St. Louis–San Francisco Railway system, and commonly called the Frisco. It helped change the region because it brought new industry and jobs for people. He pointed to the old photos of rails being laid for the trains and then to pictures of early trains that roared through Missouri with their cargo towed on rail cars.

"The population grew because people could get jobs. And with jobs, people could then build homes. They could even afford to pay to see entertainment from traveling musicians and variety shows," he explained.

"There were tent shows and carnivals and that is about the time that big traveling circuses began. From snake handlers to bearded ladies and trained animals, there was something to amuse everyone," he said.

"It was about the same time that Jacob built the Merryweather home on the land he had purchased," Audry's dad continued. "Later he passed it to his son Joseph, who passed it on to his son Benjamin, who passed it to Lincoln, your grandpa's father, and now it is owned by your grandpa, Levi. And some day, your Uncle Mike and I will continue to care for the Merryweather property. It has seen a **lot** of history," her dad said.

"And it's had a **lot** of owners," Audry said, a bit overwhelmed with all of this new information.

"Yes. And one of the best stories passed down to my father was about when his great-grandfather Joseph went to the <u>1904 World's Fair</u> held right here in St. Louis. That was quite an event. It was also known as the <u>Louisiana Purchase Exposition</u>. It showed the best of business, entertainment, and inventions from 62 countries. The news at the time said that well over 19 million people attended," he said, as Audry's eyes grew wider and wider.

From a staircase in the museum, a cheerful man appeared and said to her father, "Hi, I am Ray Goodman, your dad's friend."

They shook hands and Audry's dad thanked him for taking time to look at what he had found. Audry's excitement grew as Mr. Goodman took the wooden box into his office to examine it more closely.

Audry fidgeted and could not contain her excitement about the mystery of the bucket. Her mother finally said, "Audry, maybe we should go for a little walk and find a snack while your father is visiting with the director."

"How long are they going to be?" Audry asked with impatience.

"Now Audry, if I knew that, we would not need to go for a walk," her mom replied.

Reluctantly, Audry followed her mother out the door and down the street to look at some of the stores in the area for souvenirs to take back to California. They walked through an old neighborhood filled with quaint shops, bought some pieces of pottery from a local artist, and stopped for a treat of freshly made, frozen custard.

Finally Audry could no longer contain her impatience and asked, "Mom, don't you think we need to go back now? Dad probably wonders where we went."

"Okay. They should be finished by now," her mom agreed.

Entering the museum, Audry spotted her dad standing next to the receptionist's desk talking to Mr. Goodman and ran to his side.

"So, what **is** this?" Audry immediately asked, motioning to the box.

Civil War Relics

"Mr. Goodman's technician finally got the top off the bucket, and I'll explain to you what I learned once we leave," her dad said.

Her dad thanked Mr. Goodman's receptionist, picked up the wooden box, and headed to the car.

Once inside the car, Audry was quite annoyed, and asked, "Dad, what is *it*?"

"Mr. Goodman told me it *is* a bucket, and it *is* a collector's item. It's from the Civil War time," he said, expecting to be flooded with questions from Audry.

He was surprised when she asked, "Is that all?"

He took a deep breath and proceeded. "No, it also had inside a straight edged razor, some coins from that time in history, and a slave tag. The Civil War was a very sad time in American history when some people wanted to own other people and make them work their large properties. Other people in the country thought it was wrong to do so. That created a huge conflict between the people in America that became known as the Civil War.

"Those people who were owned by others were known as 'slaves,' and they were sometimes identified by metal tags that they wore on small chains or leather strings around their necks. Mr. Goodman thinks that the bucket was probably left behind by an escaped slave who was traveling to states that allowed them to be free. The bucket was used to carry water. And, the razor was for shaving or maybe just a keepsake.

"The part of the property where we found the bucket was thought to be part of what was known as the Underground Railroad. That was a safe route the slaves used to travel to either Kansas or Illinois where they could be free. Missouri during the Civil War was mixed. Some people were for slavery, but the majority of the population was very opposed to it. But Mr. Goodman said it truly is a solid piece of history. It is not just a story," her dad said quietly.

Stunned by this very long explanation, Audry was very thoughtful. Finally she asked, "Well, can we keep it?"

"Honey, it actually belongs to your grandfather, and he may have other ideas," her dad explained. "But I would guess he would want to keep it along with some of his other heirlooms. It **is** part of the Merryweather homestead."

"Well, okay, but I hope we can see it when we visit again," Audry said.

"I'm sure you will," he assured her.

Then, to change the mood, he suddenly burst out singing the ballgame song at the top of his lungs. Audry shrieked with laughter and began kicking her feet in a fluttering motion out of excitement. Her mother looked at the two of them and smiled. She seemed glad they were making new memories in her home state of Missouri.

CHAPTER 5

LORAL COUNTY GREW AND CHANGED through the years, as did Audry. But, Echo Woods stayed pretty much the same.

Audry's grandparents both passed within a couple of years after Audry turned 13. Her dad and Uncle Mike agreed to hire caretakers for the homestead and would meet there for brief vacations from time to time. They kept it in the family as their father had requested and even added to the size of the property when they bought 100 acres that joined the Merryweather homestead. The land had been the original site of the old Loral County fairgrounds. Even Audry remembered the festivities that occurred there when she was very young.

The fairgrounds was where people had celebrated the best of Loral County at the beginning of fall. Prizes were awarded for the best in handicrafts, produce, and even the fastest pig in the pig races. Her grandfather had been one of the judges in many events. But the best part was when her dad would take her high up in the Ferris wheel where she could see the whole countryside. Then once back on the ground, he would buy her a honey cake with pineapple whip before they walked home.

Back in California, Audry grew tall and lean, and sported a year-round tan from surfing and playing in the sun. She also enjoyed spending time with her mom and dad on movie locations and watching her dad perform daring stunts for movie productions. He managed to create excitement wherever he went.

However, the good times came to an end when Audry turned 17. Her mother suddenly became ill and passed away. Her dad's work schedule increased, and they both decided it would be best if she could live with her mother's mother, Grandma Lenzie, in Jefferson City, Missouri.

It was a different type of life for her, but she adjusted well. She went from surfing the ocean to water skiing with new friends on freshwater lakes. In school, she won medals for her competition in track, swimming, and tennis, and enjoyed participating in musicals and plays. Most of all, she looked forward to her dad's visits and watching baseball games in St. Louis or Kansas City.

Once Audry graduated from high school, she went to work for a government agency as a legal assistant in Jefferson City. She developed a deep interest in helping people with their legal problems. From time to time, she thought about going to law school and becoming an attorney like her grandfather, who had eventually been elected a Loral County judge.

Those thoughts were abruptly interrupted by yet another tragedy when her father was killed in a movie stunt accident. This created another big change in Audry's life when she inherited her father's share of the Merryweather homestead just after she turned 20.

Her Uncle Mike came home for an extended stay and spent time with Audry discussing her plans and helping her make important decisions for her future. One big responsibility she had not expected was taking full ownership of the Merryweather homestead. Uncle Mike had decided that since he was now married and living in Costa Rica, he wanted Audry to have his share of the family homestead.

She would be a part of making history here as well. She would be the first female owner of the Merryweather family homestead in Echo Woods.

With little hesitation, she took a new job near Echo Woods with the Loral County legal aid office, and moved several hours south of Jefferson City to a place she dearly loved.

CHAPTER 6

THE NEXT DAY IN THE early hours of the morning after Sam first visited Audry, she was rudely awakened from a sound sleep. There was loud laughter, talking, hammering, and singing. It was barely dawn!

Audry jumped out of bed, ran to the back of the house, and looked out the kitchen door to investigate the racket that had awakened her.

Still half asleep, she could not believe her eyes. The back property and barnyard were filled with activity and a colorful assortment of individuals carrying lumber, sawing boards, hammering, painting, and repairing the barn and outbuildings.

Strange vehicles were parked on the property between the barn and other buildings that still held some of the lumber and materials. She remembered seeing similar vehicles near the military base where she lived as a child. But, the ones near the barn had huge tires and were painted primarily a drab olive green.

As she looked around, she could see about six people hoeing and pulling weeds. Large mounds of new black dirt had been dumped in several locations, and the workers were spreading it with rakes and shovels all over the garden area. They were talking and laughing and apparently enjoying their work.

And, no surprise, at the center of all of this activity was Sam, directing all who were present and writing on his very small notepad.

She quickly changed into her work clothes and marched outside to see exactly what was taking place. She was barely outside when Sam cheerfully hollered at her.

"Hi-ho, Miss Audry, top of the mornin' to ya!" He then eagerly motioned for her to join him in the center of the barnyard.

Audry, unsure of the situation, hesitantly moved toward Sam.

"Look at what we've done, Miss Audry." Sam proudly swept his arm, pointing out the new shingles that covered the old barn roof. The fresh dark red paint that had been applied to the upper, wooden part of the barn made it stand out in the early morning light. She also noticed lumber and materials stacked in piles that would be used to repair the other buildings.

Audry was still groggy and not fully awake. "Isn't it a bit early, Sam?" Audry asked quietly.

"Oh, time is meaningless when you love what you're doing, Miss Audry. Why, we're usually up to speed long before most people get up!" Sam energetically responded with a satisfied smile.

Audry then noticed a long, flat wooden wagon nearby, with seven older women who were preparing food. They were dressed in colorful clothes that did not match, and several had bright kerchiefs tying up their hair. Others wore kerchiefs loosely draped around their necks.

Next to the wagon were three metal stands that held fuel tanks. Two heated very large black griddles on top. The women were laughing and talking while cooking an endless supply of pancakes and eggs on the griddles. The third stand held an enormous blue camping coffee pot that gave off the aroma of fresh-brewed coffee. Along with all of the food and coffee, a five-gallon crock of drinking water with a long-handled dipper sat at the end of the wagon.

The smell of the fresh food was irresistible, and Audry asked Sam, "Do you always bring your cook crew with you?"

"Well, Miss Audry, my friends and I love to eat. You know hard work makes us hungry," Sam said. "And Miss Lucy and her six sisters love nothing more than to cook and tell stories, so we all benefit," he continued.

"We're almost ready to have some breakfast before we finish for the day. Would you like to join us?"

Audry was dumbfounded about how much had been accomplished by Sam and his people. It was all too much to comprehend at once. But she couldn't refuse the invitation to eat, because that would be impolite. They had brought the grand old barn to life again with fresh paint, glistening in the morning sun. And, last, they crowned it with a brand new roof. Soon new paint would brighten the old outbuildings. She could see that Sam meant what he had said about a lot of repairs needing done to the Merryweather property.

She replied, "Well, that sounds nice. And, the food smells simply delicious."

Sam said, "Great! First of all, I want to introduce you to my friends."

The workers, as if on cue, lined up next to Sam so that he could properly introduce them. Sam said, as he gestured toward a very tall, big man who was bronzed from working in the sun for a long time, "This is Deezle. He has great strength and can reach tall places that I cannot."

Deezle looked at Audry and broke into a smile that matched his size, revealing beautiful white teeth. In a very deep, but kind and soothing voice, Deezle said, "Really nice to meet you, Miss Audry," and nodded his head toward her.

Sam next introduced a short man with lively, mischievous blue eyes. Large ringlets of blonde hair topped his head. "This is Pop. He is the caretaker for our magnificent Missouri mules. See them over there?" Sam asked as he waved in the direction of two large dark animals. "You know, they are our state animal."

One grazed nearby on new spring grass, and the other drank water from a large wooden bucket. For a moment, one stopped eating, looked at Audry and gave the quaint mule call—half horse "whinny" and half "hee-haw" like a donkey—and seemed to blink both eyes at her.

That was the first time Audry had actually seen a mule this close. They were big, to say the least, and she was very cautious.

Pop grinned from ear to ear and said, "Hello there, young lady!"

Audry shyly smiled in response, and said, "Hello, nice to meet you."

A feisty little old man with a strange felt hat with a pointed top walked toward Sam and said, "Don't forget me, Sam," then took off his hat and acknowledged Audry with a nod of his head.

Sam said, "Oh, yes, this is our water man, Clyde, Miss Audry. He is our water wizard. If he can't find water for wells and fix pumps, nobody can. He says he can 'hear' the water flowing underground, and that is how he locates the sites for wells. And, by the way, you have a working pump now in your barn, thanks to Clyde. There will be fresh water for your garden and more than enough for any animals that may need a drink."

Quickly, before Audry could ask questions, Sam drew her attention to the people working in the garden area. She now saw they had significantly expanded the garden spot and had inserted herb plots made of two-foot-square wooden forms. They had also erected white, one-foot-square cubes with round, half-dollar-sized holes on tall poles. They rose about 13 feet above the ground and proudly stood guard on each for the four corners of the garden.

Pointing to the white boxes, Audry asked, "What are those?"

"Oh, they are birdhouses specially made for the <u>martins</u>. They are our natural insect predators, so that you will not have to use dangerous pesticides that destroy bees or butterflies needed to pollinate all the crops and flowers in Loral County. The martins are your best friends for dealing with pesky insects," Sam explained.

Sam then led Audry to an area where workers were clearing the ground of dead grass and brush. "They're going to plant a large garden. You won't believe the produce they can grow," Sam explained.

As Sam pointed out the garden area to Audry, the gardeners broadly smiled at her. He then waved his arm in their direction and said to Audry, "They can grow just about anything."

"Before long, there will be enough fresh vegetables to feed everybody you know and then the rest can be preserved for food throughout the winter months," Sam said with a chuckle. "And not only that, we have planted seeds that will produce plants to attract more butterflies and bees than you have seen in a very long time. Also, you will have every kind of herb and spice for cooking or making natural remedies for whatever ails you!" Sam proudly exclaimed.

The list of plants seemed endless. With each name, Audry's eyes grew bigger and bigger. It was simply too much information to absorb this early in the morning, at least for Audry.

Sam then announced very loudly, "Now, everybody, let's eat!"

The group immediately headed to the flat-bed wagon. They took plates of eggs with pancakes and syrup, grabbed cups of coffee, and then sat on the ground. There the chatter and laughter continued.

While the workers ate, Sam introduced Audry to the seven sisters who had cooked the food. Sam explained, "Our group stumbled across the sisters over in Jasper County at a multi-church gathering. It was one of those 'all-day-meetings-with-lunch-on-the-ground' events. They were doing the cooking at the time for the traveling preacher at his big tent revivals."

As Sam said their names, each sister smiled and nodded at Audry, "They have said they might be interested in finding somebody to write a cookbook of their favorite recipes, Miss Audry. It probably will never get finished, though, because they get distracted telling stories." Then he giggled, and the sisters did as well. It was obvious he liked teasing them, and they didn't seem to mind.

"Yes, the sisters liked cooking for the revival congregations, and everything was going along just fine until the preacher bumped his head in a freaky fall. Although the doctors said he was alright, he became afflicted with a rare and unusual case of the 'blurts.' He'd be delivering a sermon at a feverish pitch and then out of nowhere he would blurt out a stream of swear words in the middle of a sentence! The words he spewed would have made a sailor blush.

"Oh, the chaos *that* created! Some claimed it was the work of the devil. Others suggested it was a hex that had been put on him by an old voodoo lady who lived deep in the woods, because the preacher had jilted her daughter.

"Needless to say, his attendance immediately dropped. Actually, people were seen running as fast as they could from his tent meetings, or stopping to cover the ears of any youngster within reach. Poor fella. But, there was a bright side to all this. He ended up singing with a country band in Branson, because the only time he didn't blurt was when he was singing.

"Anyway, the sisters came to work for us after the preacher became a country singer. Our folks loved their food, funny stories, and songs, and the sisters couldn't refuse our company and adventures. Best of all, they keep everybody happy and well fed," Sam said proudly.

Sam prodded Audry, "Come now, Miss Audry, the food is waiting."

Audry politely took a plate of food, and a much-needed cup of coffee, then joined Sam and the rest of his crew. She had to admit, the food was incredibly delicious and the coffee was the best she had ever tasted. It all seemed too good to be true. It also felt really good to be around happy people.

After seeing the barn's fresh new face, she was inspired to finish the rest of her indoor decorating projects. She remembered that she still needed to go shopping for the rest of her supplies.

"Sam, I am going shopping in Springfield today, and won't be back until late tonight," Audry said.

Sam replied, "That sounds great, Miss Audry. No worries here. We'll continue with our work. Just be safe in your travels. Oh, and don't forget my list of supplies I gave you. We'll see you again in a couple of days."

"Okay. Thanks Sam," Audry replied.

Audry thanked the sisters for breakfast, and then went back in the house to get ready to drive to Springfield. On the way out of Echo Woods, she thought to herself, "Grandpa would be happy about how the Merryweather homestead is returning to its original charm." This was in spite of the fact she could never tell anybody about who was actually doing the work.

CHAPTER 7

As DAYLIGHT TURNED INTO DARKNESS, one of Sam's old friends, Jacy, was busy at the other end of Loral County.

The light of the moon was perfect, as he effortlessly slipped through the night. Down pathways and then into thickets and woods, he silently wove his way through the hilly and rocky terrain.

Overhead, his ally Ruby flew in elegant dips and swoops upward as Jacy marked the trees as signposts for easier travel in the future. Marking trees like this was also known as blazing. This was done when Jacy marked a tree by chipping off a piece of its bark. Another type of marked tree had a limb secured in place so that, as the tree grew, the limb remained at an angle. These marker trees served as guideposts to direct travelers through thick woods or cleared trails. He had decided to blaze the trees at night under the moon. If he could see them at night, he could certainly see them in the daylight.

Once the blazing guides were in place, Jacy gave a red-tailed hawk screech that mimicked Ruby's, to let her know he was ready to head back home. With this signal, Ruby would continue to fly as a silent guide in the sky.

Jacy had learned his Native American lessons well. He was a superior scout who moved quietly and swiftly, exploring the land for new creeks or streams. Regardless of the natural habitat —rocks, creeks, cliffs, rivers, woods with thick underbrush, or even small open spaces with prairie grass that had never been disturbed—Jacy connected to the Earth and moved effortlessly. He loved the land, and knew it as well as a family member.

He had explored Missouri from border to border of adjoining states, either by land or by crossing its two big rivers—the Missouri and the Mississippi. He saw that the state had ties to many cultures from bordering states—Iowa to the north, Arkansas on the south. And across the Mississippi River to the east, Missouri was bordered by Illinois, Kentucky, and Tennessee. On the west, the state was bordered by Kansas and Oklahoma, and even Nebraska in the far northwest corner across the Missouri River. Its nickname was the "Show Me State" but it also had been called the "Mother of the West." This came from its role in the country's expansion westward, because of the <u>Pony Express</u> that had begun in St. Joseph, Missouri.

Jacy was a descendant of the <u>Cherokee</u> tribe of Native Americans that migrated from the South to the West at a very challenging time of American history. His most recent ancestors were part of the population that journeyed west on what is known as the <u>Trail of Tears</u>. Jacy's family actually settled not too far from the trail near Wilson's Creek in Missouri, where a village of tribal members had lived for thousands of years before colonists ever arrived in America.

His chosen Native American name, "Jacy," meant "moon" because he could always be present but silent. This suited him well. Although Jacy was not much of a talker, he communicated with Ruby and was a good listener. He listened to nature—the wind, animals, and streams—and to people. This was an especially valuable trait in his work at the Loral County facility for foster children—River City.

Jacy and Ruby shared a strong bond. Ruby, a red-tailed hawk, was rescued by Jacy after being wounded by hunters who had shot her for target practice several years ago. Jacy came upon the scene, just after the incident, collected Ruby, and rushed her immediately to the medicine woman with his people. She, with the assistance of Jacy, spent several weeks nursing Ruby back to health.

Once Ruby was able to fly again, Jacy took her out to the woodlands and fields to help her reunite with her flock and natural habitat. But at dusk, as Jacy was returning to his community, Ruby flew overhead and refused to stay behind.

Jacy

Jacy was puzzled about how to help Ruby find her real home. So, he decided to seek advice from a good friend, who could communicate with animals and was committed to helping them live in a world free of cruelty, neglect, and harm.

He set out on foot early one morning and traveled nearly a day to the extreme northern part of Loral County to a very old cemetery that had rarely seen a live person in almost a half century.

Jacy finally emerged from the woody underbrush onto a long forgotten pathway that led to the edge of the cemetery. Faded tombstones and crumbling statues stood guard over the dearly departed who had passed decades ago. Dates on some of the stones indicated that those souls had been laid to rest well over a century ago. Old cedar trees were interspersed with hickories, red maples, dogwoods, and woody vines to form a makeshift boundary for the cemetery. Only birds and squirrel chatter broke the peace of a now very isolated site.

Although it was very old, it was surprising how well kept it appeared. On the pathways between the tombstones, a new season of wildflowers and herbs was emerging.

Somebody had transformed an otherwise abandoned cemetery into an energy orchard. A series of raised solar panels bordered the outside perimeter, and several nearby wind turbines stood sentry over the area where a steep ravine dropped below. They were kept busy transforming a steady breeze into energy.

Standing at the very northwest edge of the cemetery was a quaint, small, old stucco building. Atop its steeply pitched roof, a metal weathervane slowly moved, telling the directions of the wind. Nearby, in full sun, stood a short stone pillar topped with a marble sundial with hour marks etched by its sculptor. Further north stood a tall, newer building with a cluster of antennas on the roof.

Jacy quietly approached the stucco building and lightly knocked on a wooden door with a rounded top. There was no response, but that was not unusual. The proprietor of the cottage was sometimes hard to find.

He noticed a wooden box next to the side of the door, marked "NOTES." As he was looking inside the box for paper and a pencil, the door slowly opened, and a smiling cheery face looked out.

Gravedigger's Cottage

Jacy politely said, "Good morning. I hope I am not bothering you, but I have come to see you about my hawk. I will appreciate it very much if you can tell me what to do, Sam."

Sam eagerly greeted Jacy and invited him inside the cottage. It was lit with sunlight that shone through leaded panes of glass and about 10 small lights that hung by silver cords from the ceiling. Ruby tightly gripped the shoulders of Jacy's leather vest with her talons. Once inside, Jacy retrieved some pieces of jerky from a leather pouch around his waist, offered them to Ruby, and coaxed her to sit on the arched back of a wooden chair.

"It's good to see you, Jacy. It has been a while. So, what seems to be the problem with this beautiful girl?" Sam asked, admiring Ruby.

Jacy told Sam about Ruby's narrow escape from death and that now she was well, she was not interested in returning to her natural habitat. She only wanted to be with him or fly above his head when he was exploring the land.

Sam chuckled and said, "She is grateful for all you have done for her, my good man. Let me visit with her while you say hello to the folks down below. You haven't been here in some time, and I think you will like our new additions."

Sam moved to the back of the cottage and lightly tapped the wall next to a calendar that hung there. Suddenly, in a split second, a large panel slid open, revealing an open area facing a heavy wooden cargo-type door that hung suspended from a rail with wheels. Stepping into the space, Sam motioned for Jacy to join him and then tapped on the panel behind him. The panel closed as fast as it had opened, and a light came on in the vacant space. Sam slid the cargo door open on its rails and stepped inside onto a platform attached to ropes on a pulley that hung from a heavy beam in the ceiling. After Jacy joined him on the platform, Sam pulled the ropes, hand over hand. As he did this, the platform slowly lowered both of them to a landing below the cottage floor.

The area had pleasant lighting, and a group of people came forward to greet Jacy. Jacy nodded his head toward the group. He knew they were Sam's friends, and he trusted Sam.

"Just stay here for a bit and visit with my friends, and I'll be back shortly," Sam instructed.

Jacy marveled at this underground community beneath the old cemetery and appreciated its fine construction. As one of Sam's friends showed him around, he saw the many sky tubes and hanging lights that provided lighting throughout. The temperature was a perfect 72 degrees, as indicated on the wall-mounted weather station.

Massive oak beams supported the area between the cement floor and the ceiling that was painted a soothing pale bluish green. The side walls were also supported with wooden beams and stucco. The walls were painted like murals, showing key events in Missouri history, of animals, trains, boats, and celebrations.

One wall was painted only with animals—mainly dogs and cats. Several "little people" sat on wide boards supported by two large ladders. There they painted more animals. No two were alike.

In the main area were heavy oak chairs and couches with large cushions. A number of wooden tables offered dining space or work areas for those who lived in this underground community. Smaller tables and chairs were arranged in various locations that would seat shorter people. Altogether, the main area could hold a very large gathering of people.

Leading off the center area, there were long hallways going in several directions, with doors that looked like hotel rooms.

As Jacy looked on from the other side of the common area, a tall, smiling older lady walked toward him from a very large kitchen area. She had come from what looked like a restaurant kitchen with a commercial cooking stove, a grill, and lots of floor-to-ceiling shelves with very large cans of food. She handed him a cup of fresh-brewed coffee and a plate of angel food cake with pink icing. He remembered this lady from another visit to see Sam long ago.

Jacy accepted the food and said, "Thank you, Miss Lucy." He took a sip of the coffee and a bite of the cake. It was very delicate with an unusual flavor. Sitting on an overstuffed cushion, Jacy enjoyed the tasty treat and a much-needed rest from a long trip.

Before long, Sam reappeared from above, carrying Ruby on his small, leather-gloved hand.

Looking at Ruby, Sam said, "I had a little visit with Ruby, and she is a very special red-tailed hawk. She wants to protect you and lead you during your travels and help you locate other animals that have been wounded and in need of special care like you gave her. She is an amazing raptor, Jacy, and we need to talk about working together to make this happen."

Sam continued, "She is truly one of our new best friends, Jacy."

Sam nodded his head first to Ruby and then to Jacy. Ruby took one hop and landed on Jacy's shoulder.

Sam then invited Jacy to follow him to see the new quiet room that had been added since Jacy's last visit. Walking together down a long hallway, Jacy observed a large area that looked like a laboratory. People in lab coats were busy measuring powders that they had ground with a mortar and pestle. Many floor-to-ceiling shelves lined the walls and contained a vast assortment of containers of liquids, powders, and wrapped herbs. They held large crocks on the bottom, and the rest of the shelves were stocked with all shapes and sizes of boxes and bottles. The bottles were green, brown, pink, clear, and blue, and each was neatly labeled with its contents.

"Jacy, here you see we have added a large quantity of natural remedies that we make," Sam said. Jacy could see smaller individuals like Sam, busy at lab tables using mortars and pestles to crush flowers and plants into fine powders. A couple of others were focused on writing in large ledgers and journals.

Pointing to two individuals working at a lab table, Sam said, "There are Izzy and Santos who are in charge of all medicines and remedies. They are writing down their diagnoses and formulas for every animal that they have treated, and noting how well they have responded to treatments and remedies. This helps their assistants in treating other similar cases. Once the animals have been given a clean bill of health by Izzy and Santos, they can be adopted into their selected forever homes."

"Their most recent cure was helping a circus elephant regain its memory," Sam said proudly.

Sam explained that Izzy and Santos were brother and sister that had previously worked as veterinarians for a major circus, caring for the animals. They left after reporting mistreatment of the animals to the Humane Society in Georgia and managed to escape with their lives after the owners threatened to kill them. Here they worked for Sam and his team in rescuing or healing animals that had been put in harm's way by heartless humans.

In an adjoining room, Jacy saw workers who were either sorting and cutting fabric or sewing pieces of cloth into checkered squares at one of several sewing machines. It was a regular assembly line of production.

"Here is our sewing room where we make bandages for injured animals. Or we recycle used clothing and remake them into blankets for warmth or rag rugs where they can rest," Sam explained.

Jacy followed Sam as they entered a large open area with several skylights, a natural rock reflection pool, and people who surrounded it reading or writing at small tables or napping in over-stuffed lounge chairs. It was all quite comfortable and serene.

Smaller rooms overlooked the main area. Through the glass in the doors, Jacy saw people singing in one room, and a person was playing a violin in another. The surrounding walls of the conservatory area contained massive shelves filled with books and a selection of musical instruments.

"This is where everyone can relax and take mental vacations," Sam explained.

"Oh, and we increased our solar energy system last year and now have electricity to power our new laboratory and many other areas of our community," Sam proudly stated. "Headstones offer perfect locations for small collectors, and our 'dearly departed' up above simply do not mind," Sam said, as he chuckled.

"So, Jacy, I think it is time we have a visit and see how we can work together to make the world more humane for all living things.

Your girl Ruby tells me that there are a lot of animals that could use our help," Sam suggested.

Jacy nodded in agreement and smiled at Sam.

"It shouldn't take long, and I will ask Deezle, Izzy, and Santos and a couple of others to join us for a little meeting," Sam said.

Together they walked into a meeting room with maps and charts on the walls, and Sam asked Gloria, his community manager, to please ask Deezle and others to join them. In the corner, a large radio base station sat on a table next to a telephone. Gloria made an announcement over the intercom system requesting Deezle and Rescue Team One to please come to the conference room. Sam then sat at the base station and put on a headset with a microphone. He pressed a button on the station and said, "Lima Charlie Five, do you read me?"

Sam spoke into the microphone again and said, "I want you to know that my friend Jacy will be joining us in a number of future rescue operations, and he will get in touch with you later to introduce himself and his friend Ruby in person. He also may work directly with you on his own, and you two can plan how to communicate with one another." Sam explained.

"Sounds good to me. I'll look forward to meeting him here at the station. Over and out," the voice replied.

Deezle, Santos, Izzy, and several others entered the room, and Sam closed the door behind them.

Later, emerging from the room, Sam said to Jacy, "Well there you have it, and it is so good to have you on our team. There is a lot of work to be done.

"I know you have a ***long*** way back, so I will lead you now to our other entrance, Jacy. That way you can use the big trail for at least part of your way home," Sam continued.

Jacy, with Ruby on his shoulder, followed Sam down a corridor to a huge set of solid wood doors. Sam operated an elaborate set of ropes and pulleys that allowed the doors to open with little effort. Daylight flooded the corridor, and Jacy shook hands with Sam and thanked him for his time and helping him to better understand Ruby.

Stepping outside, Jacy saw that he was at the entrance of a cave mostly hidden by a thick growth of trees and bushes. It was barely visible from the wide, clean trail below. The trail, which had once served as a railroad line, had been converted into what became known as the <u>Katy Trail State Park</u>. Jacy knew the trail quite well and had traveled many of its 240 miles stretching across the state along the Missouri River. But he never knew about this opening to the world he had just left behind.

Ruby gave a quick launch, soared up in the air, screeched, and the two headed back the long distance home to southern Loral County.

PHONETIC ALPHABET

Radio calls used by military groups, citizens band radio operators, air traffic controllers, some law enforcement units, and other formal operations rely upon a common alphabet. Known as a phonetic alphabet, this language helps to make sure that common letters are understood by all parties for identifying either the caller or receiver, or for spelling important words. Following is the phonetic alphabet that was adopted by radio users in the 1950s.

A = Alpha	N = November
B = Bravo	O = Oscar
C = Charlie	P = Papa
D = Delta	Q = Quebec
E = Echo	R = Romeo
F = Foxtrot	S = Sierra
G = Golf	T = Tango
H = Hotel	U = Uniform
I = India	V = Victor
J = Juliet	W = Whiskey
K = Kilo	X = X-ray
L = Lima	Y = Yankee
M = Mike	Z = Zulu

CHAPTER 8

AUDRY SLEPT VERY LATE IN the morning after her trip back from Springfield. She awoke with the sun streaming brightly through her bedroom windows.

The shopping trip to Springfield had taken much longer than she expected. Yes, she found everything on her list, but it was Sam's list that took a lot of extra time. She only bought one item that was on his list at the big hardware store—an axe. The rest of the things that she actually found were at a natural food store and a veterinarian's office. She never did find that one item, "pine tar soap." Who uses *that* anyway?!

Audry was anxious to see the garden that was being planted when she left yesterday. It had been too late to look at it last night when she got home. It would be nice to see all the wildflowers and plants bring the place alive this year. And the thoughts of seeing <u>butterflies</u> again made her smile. She would have to try and photograph some and maybe send them to a wildlife magazine.

After eating breakfast, Audry threw on her work clothes and went outside to explore the new garden. She wanted to make a list of everything so she would know what fresh herbs would be available for cooking.

Walking outside, Audry was stunned as she looked at the massive size of the garden. She couldn't imagine how she would even begin to maintain it. Hadn't they overdone it a bit? This was more than a garden. It looked like a farm with crops!

The gardeners had expanded the garden beyond reason. "What were they thinking? I am only one person and there is no way I can keep up with this by myself." And, with that last thought, her annoyance began to rise.

There were numerous two-foot-square, wooden herb boxes planted

41

and marked with square sticks—**THYME**, **PARSLEY**, **SAGE**, **FENNEL**, **MINT**, **ROSEMARY**, **OREGANO**, and on and on.

Between the herb boxes were rows labeled with names of wildflowers and milkweed. There was *so* much milkweed! In the corners of the garden and many places in between, there were small plugs of green shoots planted in the ground. Beside each plug were sticks in the ground labeled **GARLIC**. So much garlic!!

Then there were the rows marked **GREEN BEANS**, **CARROTS**, **BEETS**, **ONIONS**, **CUCUMBERS**, **ZUCCINI**, and row upon row, labeled **CORN**.

By this time she was getting a headache. She wandered over to the other part of the garden that was behind her house and counted at least 300 tomato plants!

As she looked around to try to fully comprehend what had been planted, she noticed some small bushes that had been planted in the far corner of the garden area. She was very disturbed by all of this planting that had gone on without Sam or the gardeners even having a conversation with her about what she wanted. She was feeling really riled up now, and was going to have to have a serious conversation with Sam.

As her anger rose, she marched over to one of the bushes and bent over to read the tag hanging down very low on one of the little branches of the bush. It read **GOOSEBERRY**. She said aloud to herself, "Fercryinoutloud, *gooseberry*? Who eats these!?"

Suddenly, a solid, firm nudge to her behind sent her sprawling in the soft, freshly raked soil.

Shaken, but unhurt, Audry pulled herself up on her hands and knees, and swiftly looked back to see who or what had run into her.

There, standing face to face with her, was a tan colored mule. At least she *thought* it was a mule.

Stunned, and not knowing what to do, Audry just stared back. Was this mule dangerous or friendly? Did it bite? Or worst of all, would it kick? All she could think of was running to the house and calling Sam. He *must* know something about this, since there were two mules here yesterday, even though this one was not one of them.

Stella

So far, this huge animal was just looking at her and blinking from time to time. It did not **seem** to be a threat, but Audry could feel her heart pounding. This was the first time she had come this close to a mule. So close, she could feel its breath on her face. She wasn't about to take any chances!

Slowly, Audry inched her way to the grassy area next to the garden. She wanted to get sure footing and then make a run for the house. Of course, the mule could probably outrun her if it wanted to, but fortunately, Audry didn't know this.

Once her foot touched the grass, Audry sprinted to the house at full speed as if all the worst demons of darkness were chasing her. She hit the door, ran inside, and collapsed in a chair to try to stop shaking and catch her breath.

The first thing she did, once she collected her thoughts and summoned what strength she had left, was to fish Sam's "business" card out of her wallet.

She didn't know exactly what she was going to say to him, but she was sure he would get the message. She called the number on the card and waited for an answer.

The following phone conversation went like this:

Deputy Holiday (nonchalantly):
> "Hullo, Deputy Holiday, here. What seems to be the problem?"

Audry (sounding nervous):
> "Uh, uh, well, have I reached 417-555-7665?"

Deputy Holiday:
> "Yes, ma'm, and this is Deputy Holiday. Again. What seems to be the problem, or is this a social call?"

Audry (discovering the mule was standing and bellowing at the kitchen door):
> Audry, was shaking, but then said, "I was trying to reach, uh—this number, I guess."

Deputy Holiday:
> Okey-dokey. And, so you did. What's all that bellowing? Is there a problem?

Audry:

"Well—uh … yes. But, I don't mean to be a bother. I'm just calling a number that was on a business card that was left with me."

Deputy Holiday (long pause):

"Well, allrighty then. Do you by any chance have the name of the person that you were trying to reach?

Audry (long pause, then in a whisper):

"*Sam?*"

Deputy Holiday (also in a whisper):

"*Who?*"

Audry (loudly and firmly):

"***Sam!***"

Deputy Holiday (normal voice):

"He's not here. Nope, not here right now. Not at all. No ma'am. But, if I see him, can I give him a message from you?"

Audry (emphatically):

"Yes! You can! And, you can tell him ***this***! There is a tan mule bellowing at my kitchen door. I don't know ***what*** it is going to do next. This is utterly ridiculous, and this is the first time I have come face to face with a mule!!"

Deputy Holiday (casually, after a long silence):

"Ah, well, has the mule done any damage you'd like to report?"

Audry:

"Well, it ***did*** butt me into the ground."

Deputy Holiday (after some muffled conversation at his end):

"Can you describe this mule for me?"

Audry (her temper beginning to flare):

"IT-IS-A-TAN-MULE-AND-IT-IS-BELLOWING-AT-MY-BACK-DOOR!"

Deputy Holiday (calmly):

"Oh, okay. There's no report of any missing mule today."

Audry:

"That's not the point, Deputy. I want to tell *Sam* that I think he has a missing mule!"

Deputy Holiday:

"Oh, allrighty, then. But, I've got an idea. This will help me figure something out with this investigation. See if this particular mule will take an apple. That will help."

Audry (exasperated):

"Okay! But, I have to set my phone down. Please stay on the line."

Deputy Holiday:

"Okay, that's all right with me. That'd be fine. I'm not going anywhere."

Audry quickly found an apple in the refrigerator and rushed back to the phone, as the mule continued to bellow.

Audry (grabbing the phone again):

"Are you still there, Deputy?"

Deputy Holiday:

"Why, yes, ma'm. Didn't move. Right here."

Audry:

"Well, what do I do now?"

Deputy Holiday:

"Okey dokey. Well, you need to put the apple in the palm of your hand, and hold your hand flat and then slowly offer it to the mule."

Audry:

"Well, I'll have to put the phone down again."

Deputy Holiday (unfazed):

"Okay. I'll be right here."

Audry slowly opened the door, hoping this gesture would put an end to the calamity with the mule.

The mule looked at Audry and then blinked as she slowly offered the apple with an outstretched flat hand, just as Deputy Holiday had instructed.

Without hesitation, the mule grabbed the apple with its soft, fuzzy muzzle and began to chomp away while blinking at Audry.

Audry closed the kitchen door and ran to the phone to tell Deputy Holiday that the mule had indeed taken the apple.

Deputy Holiday:

"Oh, okay. Well, that clears things up. That is Stella."

Audry:

"*Stella?*"

Deputy Holiday:

"Oh, yeow. She used to be part of a team owned by Old Man Bitler down in Greene County. One time, he took her and the rest of the team to pull a parade float in Springfield for a college homecoming parade, and she got star struck. Yeow, she thought everybody along the parade route was waving at her. She didn't know any better, and she didn't *get* that the crowd was waving at the homecoming queen candidate on the float—*not her.* When the old man got the team back home, shortly thereafter she just took up and left! She's been on the run ever since, and nobody can catch her. She just bums food wherever. She is one of-a-kind, that Stella, and she loves it when people sing to her!"

Audry:

"Oh, *really?*"

Audry had a strange feeling that this story was not entirely true.

Deputy Holiday (matter-of-factly):

"Yeow, the cattle roundup song is probably her favorite. Anything really, as long as there's **lots** of yodeling."

Audry:

"Are you, *serious?*"

Deputy Holiday:

"Well, that's what I've heard, and nobody has said otherwise."

Audry:

"Okay! Well, tell Sam I need to see him right away to talk about this, uh, mule, or 'Stella' or whoever it is."

Deputy Holiday:

"Allrighty. Will do, ma'am. By the way, who should I say called for him, and what's your number?"

Audry:

"I'm Audry and he knows full well how to contact me!"

After she hung up, Audry was certain of a couple of things. First, somebody else knew about Sam and she *had not* imagined everything over the past few days. And second of all, things weren't always what they appeared to be. In fact, since she had moved to Echo Woods, too many things did not make sense.

Now though, the mule started bellowing again, and again, and again.

Audry muttered out loud in frustration. "What am I going to do now?" She remembered Sam had introduced her to his friend who took care of mules. Maybe he had some answers. But, first Sam had to get back with her.

The last couple of days were trying Audry's patience—a surprise garden big enough for a small town, and now a mule that kept bellowing at her back door. But, the answer to both situations were connected to, well of course, *Sam*! Where in Loral County was he?!

CHAPTER 9

Nearing sunset, Jacy changed clothes from work and headed to his mailbox. Just as he stepped outside into the fresh spring evening, Ruby screeched at him and circled above his head. Amused, he chuckled and asked her, "What are you doing, you silly girl?"

Ruby screeched again and then went through her routine to lure him into following her. She didn't quite understand that sometimes he just needed to rest and relax after work. Today had been a long day at River City. There he taught physical education and health classes, and monitored games of basketball, baseball, and other recreational activities.

Not to be ignored, Ruby screeched again, and was more persistent than normal. She must have discovered something today that disturbed her, because she seemed to be quite agitated.

"Ruby, Ruby, Ruby, what do I need to see?" Jacy asked.

Once again, she circled and swooped and screeched.

"Okay! Hang on just a minute," he implored. Quickly, Jacy ran back inside his cabin, grabbed his portable radio from the charger that Deputy Holiday had given him, changed into his field boots, and threw on a light backpack.

Ruby circled, screeched, and shot off like a rocket, making Jacy sprint to catch up. She slowed just long enough so that he could keep her in sight. He followed her for nearly a mile up to a cliff where she promptly soared into a valley below. With great care, Jacy navigated the descent over rocks and through a thicket that was just starting to leaf out. Finally at the bottom, where the land leveled off, Jacy could see in the distance an old dilapidated cabin and two rickety sheds surrounded by piles of firewood. Trees and bushes had grown over much of the firewood.

Carefully Jacy approached a large oak and stood behind it for cover until he could get a better view of the property. What had Ruby seen?

Very quietly, Ruby landed on a branch higher in the tree and waited patiently for Jacy to scout out the land and buildings. She then flew very slowly and quietly toward one of the old sheds. Jacy listened intently to find out whether the residents were home or nearby. He could not hear any voices, then Ruby screeched loudly to signal to him that everything was clear and that no other people were around.

Quickly, Jacy kicked out of his spot and ran swiftly to the location where Ruby sat on a piece of the roof. He could barely see, so he flicked on a small flashlight to look inside.

Instantly he saw the problem. A young female dog was chained to a stake in the ground. She appeared to be very weak but was able to emit a shallow whine. No water or food was in sight. Jacy had seen this many times before and knew she probably had been abandoned. He immediately radioed base camp to report the problem.

"Lima Charlie Five, this is Lima Charlie Ten. Do you read me?" he called.

There was a long stretch of silence, then Jacy repeated the call.

Finally a male voice responded, "Lima Charlie Ten, this is Lima Charlie Five, how can I help you?"

"We have a very weak dog, and I'm bringing her in. Can you alert Izzy or Santos to meet me at the shelter?" Jacy asked.

"10-4, Lima Charlie Ten," the radio caller confirmed. "Just be careful. They'll be waiting."

Jacy took a burlap wrap from his backpack and laid it flat on the ground. He then pulled a tool from a pouch and cut the chain to free the dog. After freeing her, he opened a small bottle and dribbled water into her thirsty mouth. Calming and stroking her thin head, he gently wrapped the burlap around the dog, tying the ends to his body, keeping this very frail animal close to him and giving her warmth.

He gently raised himself to an upright position and motioned to Ruby to lead the way out of the valley.

Ruby screeched, and Jacy heaved a sigh of relief knowing that soon this sweet soul would get the care she needed from Izzy and Santos. She would live to see another day.

CHAPTER 10

AUDRY HAD JUST FINISHED PUTTING new hardware on her kitchen cabinets and was admiring how nice they looked. She still needed to put together her new entertainment center and replace the lampshades on the old lamps in the living room. As she headed to her office to unpack the lampshades, she heard a knock on her back door.

"Who could that be?" she muttered. "Maybe it is somebody who knows more about the mule," she thought. The only thing she knew for sure was that the mule had not left and had been enjoying some new spring grass in the pasture behind the barn.

Audry went to the door and was surprised to see a very nice looking man in a uniform. She couldn't think of any reason for an official person to be coming to see her. Then she looked down, saw Sam, and it all started to come together.

She slowly opened the door, Sam immediately swung it open further and said, "It is so good to see you again, Audry. I want to properly introduce you to Loral County deputy sheriff and county animal control officer, Bow Holiday." With a typical Sam flare, he swept his hand toward the deputy as a way of presenting him.

Caught somewhat off guard and pleasantly surprised by this visitor with his winsome smile and enchanting blue eyes, Audry didn't know quite what to say. She stammered a bit and finally said, "Ah, well, uh, it's nice to meet you, and, uh, uh, yes, my name is Audry. Bow, did you say?"

Sam immediately answered, "Why yes, it is Bow. His real name is Rainbow, but he shortened it to Bow since Rainbow didn't sound that official for an officer of the law." He then said in a hushed tone, "Yes, his parents were 'flower children,' or as some would call them 'hippies' ya know …."

Bow graciously returned the conversation to the reason for their unannounced visit.

"Nice to meet you, Miss Merryweather. Sam has told me so much about you, and I'm glad you have resettled here in your grandfather's home. The judge was highly regarded in these parts, and many were sad to see the place empty for so long," the deputy explained.

Audry was immediately taken with the deputy's charming, friendly demeanor.

Sam immediately turned the topic to Stella. "Audry, we need to talk about Stella, and maybe we can help," Sam offered.

That was certainly good to hear, Audry thought, but she didn't know exactly what to say. She hadn't meant to take the deputy away from important work at the sheriff's office.

"That's good to hear, and after that's settled, we need to talk about this industrial-sized garden that has been planted . . ." Audry complained before being interrupted by Sam.

"Come outside, if you will. We'd like to show you something," Sam suggested.

Provoked, Audry briskly walked outside, in hopes this all would quickly be settled.

Audry was a bit befuddled by her sudden guests and found herself to be even more confused that the deputy showed up with Sam. First of all, he **knew** about Sam. He not only **knew** Sam, but they appeared to be good friends. And this deputy was more like somebody you would see in the movies than in a rural community in Missouri. Handsome, friendly, and easy-going was the best she could determine about him up to this point.

Sam motioned for her to come closer to Stella, who had wandered upon the scene. Sam said to her, "Now, wait here, because this is something you don't want to miss."

Sam walked over to the sheriff's truck and slowly opened the door. Out of the back seat, a beautiful long-haired, taffy-colored dog bounded out and ran clumsily toward Stella. The mule snorted and bellowed, while the dog repeatedly leaped up and down, each time touching Stella's nose with her own. Stella knelt down and the dog eagerly licked Stella's face.

Audry was both shocked and moved at this beautiful display of affection between these two unlikely animals.

Sam finally broke the silence, saying, "Here you see the reunion of best buddies that used to live together at the farm where Stella once lived. The dog's name is Maggie, and there is so much more to the story than what Deputy Holiday told you yesterday, Audry."

Again, Sam coaxed her to come closer so he could show her something. Audry cautiously joined Sam next to Stella.

Sam pointed to some very dark ridges on Stella's back and behind her front legs. "When Stella was brought home from the parade in Springfield, her owner beat her with a wooden rod, because she had been hard for him to handle. The next day, although hurt and in pain, she found an opening in the barn and ran away. She never returned and her owner finally gave up trying to locate her."

"A couple of months earlier, Maggie had been hit by a car driven by the owner's son," Sam explained. "He wanted to hide that from his father, so he thought he would simply shoot her and tell his father that she had run away. When he went to the barn where Maggie was lying injured, Stella saw the evil look in his eye and the gun in his hand. Before he could pull the trigger, Stella kicked him into the side of the barn, knocked him out, and stomped the gun into pieces. Stella guarded Maggie and protected her from harm until Maggie was able to run away. She has been at the shelter at the sheriff's office until now."

Audry was visibly moved by this story and in a quivering voice asked, "But where will they go now?"

Sam said, as the deputy nodded, "Well, we have a lead on forever homes for them, but we need to house them in a safe and comfortable place until we can get their new owners to pick them up.

"That is where you come in, Audry. We need to borrow your barn so that they have a place to stay for a while," Sam explained.

Audry had never taken care of a large animal before—like a mule. Not to mention she was still half-way scared of Stella. Besides, she had no feed, or time to feed them. She had a full load of work assignments.

"I dunno, Sam. I don't think so. This is too much for me to take on right now," Audry protested.

"Well, there is plenty of room and water in your barn, and my people will make sure they are fed every day. We even brought grain and hay for Stella and a bag of Maggie's favorite chow," Sam said.

"Sam, I don't know anything about mules, and frankly she scares me," Audry said in opposition.

Stella was quietly sitting on her haunches. Audry looked over and saw oversized tears streaming down Stella's cheeks. Maggie began to whine and warble. Once again, Audry was overwhelmed with a situation that was not familiar.

Finally, Sam said, "There is nothing to be afraid of, Audry." He gently took her hand and laid it upon Stella's neck and helped her stroke the mule's soft ears. Stella immediately leaned into Audry and gently rubbed her chin on Audry's shoulder.

"See, she is a very sweet soul, and there is nothing for you to fear," Sam softly and gently said.

At this point, the deputy chimed in, "You would be doing a great service, Miss Merryweather, because Stella and Maggie are both in danger, if their former owner finds them. He thinks of them as dumb animals and would have no problem with disposing of them, just to prove he is all powerful."

"They will be getting a forever home, right?" Audry asked.

"That's the plan, Audry," Sam said.

"Well, I guess for now that will be okay. The barn is empty anyway. At least I think it is. I haven't been in it yet since I moved here," Audry said.

Before she could discuss this development further, Sam turned the subject to the garden or, rather, to the crops.

"And, don't worry, I will make sure that everything that has been planted will be taken care of Miss Audry," Sam assured her. "You see, it is customary in this area to do a type of sharecropping. We do the work, give you half of the produce, and we take the rest for our time and labor. The same goes for your pasture. We will bale the hay, take half for our use, and give you the other half to sell or store in your barn," Sam explained.

Audry thought for a minute and said, "That sounds reasonable to me. I know very little about gardening and do not have the extra time it would take to even begin to care for everything."

At this point, Deputy Holiday suggested that they help Stella and Maggie get settled in the barn. He also noted that they could be outside with Sam's crew of people, because the fence surrounding the barn and outbuildings had been mended. "They can get fresh air and sunshine in the daytime, and then sleep inside at night," the deputy explained.

Sam coaxed both Stella and Maggie toward the barn, as the deputy opened the door. Audry followed, wanting to see the inside of this grand old structure that she hadn't really seen in many years. Sam led both animals inside, and the deputy held open the door for Audry. Sam flipped a switch on the wall, and large hanging lamps lit up the inside. The sweet smell of clover hay filled the air, flooding Audry with many fond memories. It made her want to climb the wooden rungs to the loft and see if there were any baby kittens. But she had not seen any cats, so she knew that was highly unlikely.

Looking around, she saw that fresh straw had been hauled in and piled near a corner. Looking along the other end, she noticed that a number of three-sided, boxy structures had been attached to the wall, low to the ground, and had been filled with straw. She wondered what purpose these served but was more interested in the new pump station that sat in the middle of the barn. Next to it was a large metal tub. Sam flipped a switch next to the station and a motor whirred into action, and fresh water poured into the tub from a pipe. Immediately, Stella and Maggie began slurping and lapping the fresh sparkling water.

Audry ran her fingers through the water as it continued to pour into the tub. It was cool, clear, and smelled so pure and clean. "What a wonderful thing to have on my property! Fresh water, and I don't have to pay a city utility to use it. This is truly amazing," she thought.

The deputy left and shortly returned carrying a large bag of dog food and a flat round food tray. Ripping open the bag, he poured some of the food into the tray and Maggie licked his hand and started nibbling at the chow. He left again and returned with a bag of grain mix that he poured into a wooden box. It smelled sweet like molasses, and Stella immediately dug in the box with her muzzle and munched away. Next, he hauled in a couple of bales of hay and broke one open that Stella could eat later.

The three stood around watching the animals eat and talked about the improvements that Sam's crew had made. There were no more leaks from the old roof, and the barn was almost as strong and sound as when it was originally built. It was remarkably quiet and peaceful.

Before they left, Audry could not resist the temptation to climb the rungs along the side of one wall and peak into the loft. Once in the loft, she looked around at a few bales of old straw and spied the large door that opened out onto the barn lot below. At one time, it was used by workers during the summer to hoist hay into the loft. She unsnapped the spring lock and pushed the door open. Bright sunlight rushed in, and once her vision adjusted, she could see across the countryside as if she were a child again. She remembered riding atop the Ferris wheel at the county fair with her dad. It was pure beauty that stimulated all of her senses, and her heart filled with a joy she had not known in a very long time.

The deputy called from below, "Are you okay Miss Merryweather?"

Lost in her memories, Audry slowly replied as she smiled, "Oh, yes, I am really fine. Thank you, deputy."

CHAPTER 11

"LIMA CHARLIE ONE, COME IN ASAP," the voice implored over the radio. "This is Lima Charlie Five, come in! We have a situation." It was Deputy Holiday on the radio, and he sounded stressed, which was very unusual.

Deputy Holiday waited and then called again, "Lima Charlie One, this is Lima Charlie Five, come in."

Finally, after another minute, there was a response, "Lima Charlie One here. What seems to be the problem?" the female voice asked. Deputy Holiday recognized Gloria's voice on the radio.

"Okay, you need to call me on the land line and dispatch Rescue Team One to the shelter."

"10-4, deputy. I'm on it," Gloria responded.

Gloria wondered what had happened, but she first announced over the intercom system that there was a 10-11 at the sheriff's office and for Rescue Team One to respond ASAP. Then she punched in the numbers on the telephone to the deputy sheriff's office.

Deputy Holiday answered immediately, "Deputy Holiday here."

"This is Gloria. What's up Bow?" she asked.

"Oh, boy, Gloria, we've got a problem," the deputy said. "I got a call from Miss Aggie Larson's cousin from out of state to check on her welfare. She hadn't answered the phone in a couple of days. So I drove up to Freeman Ridge to check on her and found her in bed. Dead. Looks like old age finally got her. Last time I heard, she was about to turn 100.

"Anyway, I started looking around to see if everything was okay outside and heard the biggest ruckus I've heard in a long time. In an old building, there were all kinds of hungry cats and dogs and two lambs, and a real mess!! It hadn't been cleaned in weeks and there was no food or water. The animals are pretty lean. I ran outside and got buckets of water from the hydrant to fill some pans. Then I called Early Fink, the county coroner to take care of Miss Larson, and next I called you."

Bow continued, "Here's the deal. The shelter is completely full, and the new 'forever home' owners won't be here for a couple of days to pick up their adoptees. Where's Sam?"

"Well, he said he had to rest. He is in the conservatory playing his <u>zink</u> and said he absolutely didn't want to be disturbed," Gloria replied.

"Oh, boy," he replied. "I'm in a real bind. Before these animals can get adopted they have to come to the shelter and it is FULL!! The only place I can think of that can house the shelter animals is Miss Audry's barn. But I think her patience is worn thin with everything she has faced since moving here. I'll just have to take my chances, because all these animals need a place to stay before we can find them homes."

"Okay, I'll let Sam know that you called, Bow. Good luck and keep us posted!" Gloria replied.

Deputy Holiday pondered the situation and decided he needed to get outside and simply take a walk. Fresh air usually helped him to clear his head. But he figured this state of affairs would take a whole lot more than fresh air.

After he walked for about 10 minutes, he decided he would talk to the rescue team and have them water Miss Larson's animals, put each in its own carrier with blankets, and then transport them to the shelter. But, then, after that, he wasn't sure.

He thought, "Oh, for the love of pigs and puppies, there are so, so, many problems, and sometimes it seems like it's only me and Sam's rescue team that are trying to resolve the problems in Missouri. There are too many animals not getting proper care or are simply abandoned. And the puppy mill operators only want to make money by selling more and more puppies, some with a lot of problems. The poor mothers of those puppies were never free." His thoughts raced as he walked faster and faster.

Shortly after he returned to the office, he got a telephone call from Santos asking for further directions. Bow frankly didn't know how this was all going to turn out, but he advised Santos to stay by the phone and he would call him back later.

Bow knew that Audry might be his only hope for solving this huge problem he faced. Would she even listen to him? He just needed to borrow her barn and one of her buildings for a very short period of time. But she was a smart young woman, and he thought the best way to approach her was to talk to her in person. One thing he learned from his grandmother was that when you go visit somebody, you should take a present. But what would that be? This day was not going well, and now he had to think of this?

He knew he was really hungry and thought it wouldn't hurt to take some food, and thought Audry might like something as well. Well, it couldn't hurt ….

Stopping by Franco's Cafe, Bow ordered lasagna, salad, and Italian bread for two. He also picked up some chilled lemonade at the convenience store and headed to Audry's home.

The lasagna was the best in Loral County. But it was only available on Tuesdays as the café special on the menu.

As Bow traveled down the open road, the moon shone bright, and he smelled the ripe spring air. Soon everything would be in bloom. The air was fresh but sweet, with the scent of new leaves popping out on the trees, and also musky from fresh plowed fields that he passed on the road.

He decided to park his vehicle on the other side of the barn and quickly check out the space inside once more to make sure there was enough room for Miss Aggie's animals, *if* Audry agreed to let them stay there.

After peeking inside, Bow was satisfied that there would be enough room to house the shelter animals and still give Stella and Maggie plenty of space. Both were content in the warmth and comfort of the barn and were snuggled in a corner.

He grabbed the food bags out of the cruiser, walked up to Audry's back door, and knocked.

It took a minute or so, but finally Audry asked, "Who is it?"

"It's me, Bow. I need to talk to you, so I thought we could do that over the dinner that I brought," he rapidly said. He was quite nervous about this meeting and felt his stomach turn into a knot.

"Well, okay! Give me a second," she replied.

When Audry finally opened the door, Bow could see she was in running clothes and shoes.

With a big friendly smile, she asked, "Hi, what's going on? And, food to boot? Wow, I'm impressed. This must be important."

"Hey there, I hope I'm not bothering you. It looks like you have been working out or something," Bow said.

"Yeah, I took a run down the road earlier," she acknowledged. "The weather was perfect this evening."

"Are you hungry? I am and thought you might be as well," Bow said somewhat sheepishly. It really was a wimpy way to get to talk to Audry. But this day hadn't given him much of a chance to even breathe, let alone eat.

"Oh, okay. Sure, we can talk. You didn't have to bring food, but that was very thoughtful" she said politely.

"I brought lasagna, fresh salad, Italian bread, and chilled lemonade. How does that sound?" he asked.

"Well, I do love Italian food, but where did you find that in Echo Woods?" she asked.

"Oh, from Franco's Café. Every Tuesday, Mrs. Franco cooks Italian food using her old family recipes," Bow explained. "She knew your dad and uncle when they were boys."

"This is unexpected, but a nice surprise. I'll get some plates, forks, and glasses. Have a seat. Do you want ice in your glass?" she asked.

"Sure, thank you," he replied.

She handed Bow his glass and then sat across from him at the table. Audry took a bite of her lasagna and was pleasantly surprised at its wonderful flavor. "Wow, this is really *very* good. I had no idea about the cafe's special menu," Audry said with delight.

Audry continued, "So how was your day, Bow? I know you are very busy. This county is pretty large and has a lot of activity for a small office. I'm sure you work many hours to take care of everything that needs to be done. Something really important must have happened to make you stop by."

"So, you like the lasagna?" he asked, stalling while he mustered the courage to answer her question.

"Well, yes, it really is very good. I need to stop in there and get a menu. I could order food and pick it up on my way home from running errands," she replied.

Bow took another large bite of lasagna and chewed quietly while he pondered his current dilemma, following with a sip of lemonade to clear his throat.

"It has been a really tough day. One of our oldest residents in the county died. Miss Aggie Larson. She actually knew your grandfather. But, then again, I guess everybody in Echo Woods over the age of 50 knew your grandfather," he said.

"I'm sorry to hear that," she replied. "Not that they knew my grandfather, but that the lady passed away."

There was an uncomfortable silence, then Audry asked, "So how did this lady's passing away prompt you to come and visit me tonight?"

"Well, you might say, it is because of her—well, uh, sorta—it's the family she left behind," Bow stammered.

Audry gave Bow a skeptical look, then looked at her forkful of food and asked, "So, how does that affect me, and why do we need to talk?"

The stalling and hesitation was more than Bow could stand. He needed to find a solution for the shelter animal problem. Finally, he just laid out the problem as honestly as he could.

Gathering his last bit of courage, he poured out his story. "Audry, I am in a real bind, and I need to borrow more space in your barn until the new people come and pick up their adopted pets at the animal shelter this weekend. The shelter is overrun right now. We've got cats, dogs, guinea pigs, three rabbits, and two lambs. And Miss Larson had a lot of animals that need to go to the shelter right away. There it is. It's just that simple, and there are no other options right now. You see, the county was supposed to be building a larger shelter, but they haven't and I have more animals than Noah's ark, and frankly, I don't know what else to do!"

He continued, pleading. "I can work with Jacy and the kids at River City and they can help tend to the animals so you won't have to ...."

Audry interrupted, "Bow, I really had not planned on harboring a bunch of animals. That is a lot of responsibility. And who is Jacy? Echo Woods has a really bizarre way of welcoming new residents! Yes, Sam's people have taken care of the mule and the dog, but this is a LOT to ask, Bow!"

In an apologetic tone, Bow replied, "Audry, this doesn't look good, I know. But I don't know what else to do. I sincerely apologize for everything. Please, it would only be for three days, and you wouldn't have to do anything. Sam and his people, and Jacy and his kids would take care of everything."

"And what about the next time, and the next time, and the next time you have animals that don't have owners just yet?" she asked unfazed. She had been raised to stand her ground, and she was not giving it away now, deputy or no deputy.

She immediately wondered, though, what was it with all of the animals and no place to house them in Loral County? Something really needed to be done to expand the shelter.

Bow was tired and didn't have any fight left in him right now. He hung his head in defeat and asked if he could use her phone.

She paused for a minute and said, "Sure, you can use the one in the library." She led him down the hall, turned on the light, and showed him the phone.

As she headed back to the kitchen, she noticed lights on a vehicle slowly driving down the lane to her place. That was odd, because she wasn't expecting anybody. But then again, nothing really had made sense since she had arrived in Echo Woods, so why should it start now?

She waited for somebody to knock on her door, and was alarmed when that didn't happen. She began putting dishes away and tidying the kitchen. Suddenly two men burst through her kitchen door and started leering and shouting at her. They stunk like they had not bathed in months and had scraggly beards and long greasy hair.

She loudly yelled at them and demanded, "Who are you and what do you want!!?"

The much bigger one grabbed her arm and, with a terrifying sneer, he spat while whispering in her face, "We want our mule, and we know you have her!!!"

She twisted her arm and body trying to escape his grip and shouted at the top of her lungs, "I don't know what you're talking about!"

Then the shorter one yelled, "Yeow, we heard that dumb animal was seen around here, and we decided to check it out for ourselves! And, what do ya supposin'— we saw her in your barn?!? That mule ain't yorn, an' you need to learn a lesson about that!"

"No, you don't understand!" Audry cried.

At that point, the bigger man said, "We'll see about that!" and raised his hand to strike her.

Before he could land a blow, a loud electric buzz jolted the air. The bigger rube screamed and fell to the floor. Out of nowhere, Bow had slipped into the room and had tasered the cretin, bringing him down before he could hit Audry's head.

Immediately, Audry's adrenaline kicked in, she sprang out of the kitchen, ran to the living room, and retrieved an old shotgun that hung above the fireplace. She cocked the old 12 gauge into action and prepared to shoot if either man came after her.

Looking into the kitchen, she saw that Bow had everything under control. He had immediately cuffed the man he had tasered. The other one was begging and crying for mercy. Bow cuffed him as well and ordered them both to lie down while he radioed for backup.

Just to make sure, Audry marched into the kitchen with the shotgun pointed at them and angrily stared at the two men.

"Sheriff's on his way," Bow assured her.

Then he angrily barked, "The Bitler boys have been bullies in this county for a long time, and that time just ran out!"

He gently removed the shotgun from Audry's firm grip. She leaned against the wall to support herself. Everything that had just occurred was beginning to sink in, and she was beginning to shake. Angry tears filled her eyes. Bow patted her on the back and assured her everything would be okay.

CHAPTER 12

AFTER THE SHERIFF ARRIVED, BOW helped to load the Bitler brothers in the cruiser. Once the sheriff drove way, Bow went to his vehicle and retrieved a leash and collar from the trunk. Then he went to the barn, petted Maggie, and put the collar and leash on her. Talking to her gently, he led Maggie back to Audry's kitchen.

Audry sat in a rocking chair in the living room past the kitchen. She was quiet as she slowly rocked in the chair.

Bow walked over to the chair with Maggie, who was slowly wagging her tail. Maggie sat down in front of Audry and looked up into her face.

"I'm so sorry about those scoundrels," Bow tried to reassure Audry. "This simply is not how things go around here, and normally people don't have to worry about fools like the Bitler brothers. The good news is they will probably be going away for a while. They've been on the wrong side of the law for years."

"I don't know what I would have done if you hadn't been here," Audry said, still in shock. "I just don't understand how things could have been so boring when my dad and uncle lived here, and now it seems like there is some kind of drama every day!"

"Well, I have to admit, before you arrived, it was pretty dull," Bow acknowledged.

"Anyway, I think it would be a smart idea for you to keep Maggie inside the house with you," Bow instructed.

As he said her name, Maggie wagged her tail and stood up.

Maggie

"She is an excellent watch dog and will let you know if anybody comes near your house. I'll make her a bed on your back porch if you like. She has been housebroken, so there shouldn't be a problem with accidents."

"No, she is welcome to stay inside. It is going to take me a while to get over this night, and I think we will get along okay," Audry agreed.

Bow stroked Maggie on the head and talked to her. Then he took Audry's hand, and placed it on Maggie's head as they patted her together. Maggie wagged her tail, looking at Audry's face and then at Bow's eyes. She laid her chin on Audry's knee and softly whined as if she were trying to reassure Audry.

Bow pulled away and went to retrieve the old shotgun lying on the kitchen table. On his way to put it in its place, he said to Audry, "You *do* know that this gun is harmless, don't ya?"

"What do you mean?" she asked, concerned.

"Well, it has no shells in it. No ammo," he flatly explained.

"No!" Audry exclaimed.

"Yes, it is uh, well, uh, a nice decoration I guess, but that is about all it is …."

That was too much for Audry to think about tonight. "I don't even know who it belonged to, and it's ugly, besides!! I don't want to think any more about what *could* have happened here tonight!!"

"I totally understand, and it might be a good idea just to put it away in your attic as a keepsake. It's probably not very accurate anyway," Bow advised.

Audry, expressing her sincere appreciation to Bow, said, "I really don't know how to thank you for being here tonight. I hate to think what might have happened if you hadn't stopped in."

Bow said, "I was just doing my job, but I am glad I was here also. Still, I could use your help for a day or two, because of the extra animals from Miss Larson's place. The animals at the shelter will have forever homes soon, and they are all in good health. Izzy and Santos took care of spaying and neutering them and giving them their shots. It is just that you have this incredible barn and an empty building that could give these animals a temporary home, and the kids at River City would love caring for them."

Bow continued his plea for help. "You would be doing a great service to the animals ***and*** the River City kids. You might also enjoy seeing how happy those animals make those kids."

Audry was tired, still in something of a daze, and she had no energy to continue resisting his request.

"Oh, all right," she finally said. "As long as the kids are supervised, the animals are fed and watered, and I don't have to wrangle a mule, I guess it will be okay until you get the other animals rescued and treated."

Bow breathed a sigh of relief and said to Audry, "Well, this means more than you know. How about I take us to a real Italian restaurant this Saturday? It's the least I can do. I have to go pick up new uniforms in Springfield on Saturday, and I think you could use a change of scenery."

Audry looked at Bow and Maggie and said, "Can I get back with you on that? I am actually having a hard time believing that anything is going to be normal around here. I want to make sure that this has not been a big nightmare and a bad decision to move here!!"

"Oh, no, no, no. It's really a great place to live, and you already know how nice it can be. This is your home now, good and bad. And there are really nice people here who care about one another. I'll give you a call tomorrow. Okay?" Bow gently reassured her as he searched her face to see if she really was okay.

Audry looked at Maggie, who continued to wag her tail, and finally said, "Okay. What could possibly go wrong before then?"

CHAPTER 13

AFTER LEAVING AUDRY'S, BOW WENT back to the sheriff's office to check on the animals, meet up with the rescue team, and contact Jacy. Normally, daily activities were not so hectic in Loral County and certainly not in Echo Woods. At least the rescue team knew what to do. They had secured Miss Larson's animals in their individual carriers and placed them in a large horse trailer along with the lambs, who took turns nervously bleating.

For now, the animals would have to stay in their carriers in the horse trailer until the shelter animals could be relocated to Audry's barn.

Bow called on the radio. "Lima Charlie Ten, this is Lima Charlie Five, do you read me?" He waited for about 30 seconds and then repeated the call.

After he repeated the call several times, the radio crackled to life, "Lima Charlie Five, this is Lima Charlie Ten. I read you now. What's up?"

"Call me on the land line, Lima Charlie Ten. I need your help," Bow instructed.

In a few seconds, the phone rang, and Bow explained to Jacy about the animal rescue and that he needed help with the animal transfer from the shelter to the Merryweather property.

Jacy understood and said he was on his way.

Bow went outside and talked to Izzy, Santos, Deezle, and the rescue team. They decided to load the shelter animals in various carriers and help Jacy haul them in several utility vans to Audry's barn. While two people started loading animals, others loaded bags of cat and dog food and tubs for water into a pickup truck.

About the time they were ready to move out, Jacy arrived in

his jeep. Deezle jumped into action and helped Jacy transfer Miss Larson's animals from the horse trailer into the shelter housing. Santos would stay behind to help examine the new shelter residents and treat those needing medical attention.

At Audry's place, Bow and the rest of the team carefully unloaded the shelter animals and released them from their carriers into the remodeled barn and workshop. The dogs and lambs were housed with Stella in the barn, and the cats got free run of the converted workshop. Fortunately, the rabbits and guinea pigs had space back at the shelter.

Once trays and tubs were finally filled with food and water, Bow and the others returned to the shelter to finish getting Miss Larson's animals settled in, and making sure they had plenty of water and food. Those that might need medical treatment would be taken back to Sam's and cared for by Izzy and Santos.

Finally, a little after midnight, Bow was able to take stock of the day's events. The most unsettling part was the invasion by the Bitler brothers into Audry's house. He became quite angry to think these bullies not only abused animals but treated people no differently and had gotten away with it for so many years. He was just extremely glad that Audry had not been another one of their victims.

Audry was indeed an interesting person. Independent, smart, self-assured, a natural beauty, but gutsy too—especially with a shotgun with no ammo. That made him smile and shake his head. But he was concerned that everything she had experienced so far was making her have second thoughts about living in Echo Woods. He hoped he could show her that Echo Woods indeed was a special place with a lot of really good residents—aside from the Bitler brothers.

CHAPTER 14

BY SUNRISE, JACY WAS ON his way to work and had already made plans with the River City administrator to take 10 residents to the Merryweather property. There they would care for the sheltered animals and clean the barn and workshop.

Before boarding the mini-bus, Jacy talked to the kids about what they would be doing with the animals—walking the dogs on leashes, filling water and feed containers, changing litter boxes, and cleaning out the barn.

The top question from the kids was about the animals' names.

"Some do not have names right now," Jacy explained. And then of course, a couple of kids asked if they could name them. Jacy answered, "I suppose, if you like. But, their new owners can rename them, you know."

With that, the group started chattering about the importance of names. One boy volunteered that he had given himself a new name last year. Another asked, "Why?"

"Well, I wanted to actually like the name I was being called. And you can too. If you don't like your name, you can go change it. Even if some judge doesn't approve of your name, legally, you can still give yourself a new name, and just call it a nickname," he explained.

That prompted some of the others to start thinking of new names for themselves.

"I wanna be called Kevan," one girl said.

"That's crazy," one boy immediately interjected. "That's a boy's name."

"No, it's not!" she protested. "That is a combination of my parents' names—Kenny and Vanessa! So there!"

"All right, Kevan!" the boy replied. "I like that. Then, I think I want to be called Ali, after the greatest boxer of all time!"

"Okay, Kevan and Ali," Jacy said loudly over the chatter, "we need to talk more about these animals before we get started. So, quiet down now, and listen."

Jacy talked to the kids about how to handle the animals and how to approach them calmly.

"They're already scared because of their sudden move from the shelter to Miss Merryweather's place," he said.

He discussed how to approach them without creating too much excitement.

Since the animals' new owners would be arriving in a few days, Jacy didn't foresee any real problems. He guessed that the worst challenge might be dealing with the kids in the future, because they might want to be more involved with the strays at the shelter. But that could be resolved.

Once the bus was unloaded, Jacy took five of the kids to the barn where they would tend to the dogs. The other five would go to the workshop to provide care for the cats. The next day the two groups would swap duties.

The dogs were happy to see the children. Wagging tails signaled their delight. Several ran around in circles, while others jumped and barked with excitement. The kids laughed and shouted to one another as they greeted the dogs and then patted their heads.

"Just be gentle, get acquainted, and I'll be right back," Jacy instructed. He took the other five children to the workshop where the cats were housed. Once released from their carriers, the cats wandered out and looked around at their new surroundings.

As typical of feline creatures, the cats' curiosity took over and they explored every square foot of the shop. Some of the cats even made it to the top of the rafters. Others found sunny spots on the workbenches and watched the antics of other cats or simply napped.

"I'll be right back," Jacy said. "I'm going to get the food from the bus." He carefully shut the door behind him, making sure that none of the cats made a break for the door.

After delivering food to both the cats and dogs, Jacy took five collars and leashes and began putting the collars on the dogs.

"We'll take them down to the corral and walk the dogs there," he instructed.

The three boys and two girls eagerly accepted the ends of the leashes, once Jacy had attached them it to the dogs' collars.

"Now, you have to hold on to the leash really tight. We can't let them get away," he cautioned.

The dogs could sense they were going outside and tugged and pulled on the leashes.

Jacy said, "Now hold tight, and go down through the walkway to the front of the barn while I close the gate behind you."

With this, each of the five children led one dog in a line toward the front door. Once outside, with Jacy's help, they walked the dogs to the corral. Following the group, of course, was Stella, whose curiosity could not be contained.

One by one, each child and dog entered the corral through a gate. A couple of the dogs were really excited at the feel of freedom and wanted to jump and run. Fortunately, each young person held on tight to the leash. Everybody got a good workout and fresh air.

They ran and walked the dogs for about half an hour. Jacy then instructed the kids to take this group of dogs back to the barn and return with the others, so they could get exercise as well.

Finally, after exercising the dogs and feeding Stella and the lambs, it was time to join the rest of the team at the workshop.

After a while, Jacy gathered the kids back into the barn to ask if there were any questions. After looking at dark clouds that began roiling in the sky, Jacy said, "We'd better head back. It's going to rain soon."

"No!" some protested.

"Just a little longer," another one pleaded.

"No, we have to be back by noon," he instructed. "You'll get to see them tomorrow."

"After this week, will we get to see them again sometime?" a small girl quietly asked.

"I don't know, but probably. Maybe we can have Deputy Holiday bring several dogs to River City and you can spend time with them there. I'll talk to him about that," he said.

Suddenly a bolt of lightning exploded nearby, hitting the ground. The kids shouted, screamed, and ran as fast as they could for the bus.

Before heading back to River City, Jacy jumped in the driver's seat and grabbed his clipboard from the dash of the mini-bus to make some notes to himself. He glanced at the list, and then at the faces of the kids in his rearview mirror as it began to rain.

Jacy stood up, faced the children, and with a puzzled look on his face asked, "Where's Django?"

The kids looked up at Jacy with blank faces.

Jacy then calmly asked, "Does anybody have an idea where he might be?"

The bus remained silent as a couple of the boys squirmed. This was not unusual, because they could never sit still under any circumstances.

After waiting for a few minutes while looking at each one individually, Jacy finally said, "Okay, gang. We need to go back to the barn and see if we can find him. If he's not there, I'm going to have to call the authorities and file a missing person report."

"Is he in trouble?" a boy asked in a worried voice.

"Well, he could be if he ends up with the wrong people," Jacy quietly but sternly responded. "That's why we need to go look for him. Now!"

CHAPTER 15

IT HAD BEEN A STRUGGLE for Audry to fall asleep the night after the Bitler brothers' invasion, even though Maggie hovered nearby. Did Maggie sense the danger that she had escaped the night before? Audry wasn't sure. But Maggie seemed very smart and alert to everything around her in Audry's home.

To make up for lost sleep, Audry gave herself permission to take a mid-morning nap. She was finally sleeping when the telephone woke her close to noon. Picking up the phone on her nightstand, she groggily answered, "Hello?"

"Oh, Audry? Are you okay?" Deputy Holiday asked.

"Yes, I am just a bit tired, because I didn't sleep well last night," she admitted. Then she added, "But I had Maggie to keep me good company."

"Oh, okay. That's good to hear. Everything else okay around there? No stray mules, giraffes, ostriches, or other wildlife?" he teased.

"No, thankfully, it is very peaceful this morning. I did see Jacy with the River City kids earlier tending to the animals. No drama *yet* today, and I certainly hope it stays that way!" she replied.

"Well, I wanted to ask you again to ride with me Saturday to Springfield to pick up my new uniforms," he said.

She didn't answer right away, and there was an awkward silence. She then asked, "You're absolutely sure this is not going to end up being some kind of animal rescue mission?"

Bow burst out laughing. He was surprised by Audry's pointed question. "No, no, no, none planned. I am just going to pick up my new uniforms and take you to one of my favorite restaurants. The people who own it are very nice, and the food is the best. You have been so generous about letting the animals stay at your place. It's the least I can do, and I'd like to drive you around Springfield so you can see some new places to shop."

Audry smiled and thought it would be good to see something new. She really had not had time to get acquainted with too many new people yet in Echo Woods, let alone Loral County. And Springfield was really a nice city.

"Well, okay, I think I can handle that," she said with a lilt in her voice. "What time should I be ready?"

"I'll pick you up at 9 o'clock," Bow said.

"Well, okay. I guess I'll see you then," Audry replied.

After getting off the phone, Audry thought it would be a nice change of pace to visit Springfield and try a new restaurant. It would also be nice to have somebody show her some new places.

Audry was also looking forward to visiting St. Louis, once again. Maybe she could see if there were new exhibits at the museum and check the schedule for new plays at the big theater downtown.

In the middle of her daydream, Audry was interrupted by a knock on the back door. Still uneasy from last night's drama, Audry cautiously approached the door and asked, "Who is it?"

"It's Jacy from River City, Miss Merryweather. I want to ask you a question," Jacy responded.

Slowly, Audry opened the door about two inches to peek outside. Seeing that it was a young man with a picture ID hanging from a lanyard around his neck, she opened the door farther.

"Hi, Jacy. How can I help you?" Audry asked.

"Well, the kids and I took care of the animals this morning and I just wanted to make sure that everything was satisfactory," Jacy explained. "We made sure the gates and doors were all secured when we were done, so there shouldn't be any escapees. If anything appears out of order, please call me at River City."

He didn't mention Django, because it would have been unethical to discuss anything about a resident with an outside party.

"Oh, okay. I actually have not been out to check on anything. I haven't seen anything out of the ordinary either. But if I do, I'll let you know," Audry assured him.

"Well, I know Bow really appreciates the temporary quarters. That is very generous of you," Jacy said as he began to walk away.

The kids were chattering among themselves as Jacy got back on the mini-bus.

"Okay I checked the barn again and didn't see Django. And, I talked to Miss Merryweather and she said she had not seen anything out of the ordinary. So, I need you guys to focus and think," Jacy said, somewhat annoyed. "Who was last with Django?"

"Nobody!" an older boy protested. "He stinks from that danged pouch he wears around his neck!"

"Okay, okay, that's enough, Eddie," Jacy commanded. "Just for your information, that pouch is called an <u>acifidity bag</u> and it contains a natural ground herb and other items that are special to him. Some people wear those because they think it helps to ward off illnesses among other things. It is also used as a spice in some Indian dishes. You really shouldn't judge people until you learn more about them. He is just like you, and he's just trying to make it through this life, the best way he knows how.

"Now, I want to know who saw him last? And, by the way, unless I get some answers, there is no rec time tonight," Jacy warned.

There was a unified groan, followed by complaining. One small girl raised her hand.

"Yes, Kiki?" Jacy acknowledged.

In a small timid voice she replied, "Well, when I was petting the kitty in the shop, I was looking out the window and saw that mule. And, then I saw Django walk over to that mule and talk to it."

"Oh, right!!" one boy blurted out in disbelief.

"Trevor, it's okay. Settle down. If that is what she thought she saw, then that is what she saw," Jacy said in defense of Kiki.

Kiki's small voice grew intense as she protested, "Mules know stuff. Lots of STUFF!"

"Okay, now, I'm going to have to take you guys back to River City," Jacy said. "And if anybody remembers anything that can help us find Django, please let me know."

CHAPTER 16

As SOON AS JACY PARKED the mini-bus at River City, he met with the administrator to share the news of Django's absence. He volunteered to meet with Deputy Holiday to file a missing person report and discuss possible methods for finding Django before he had time to get too far out of the area. Jacy hoped that his travels had been delayed because the rain shower had turned to a heavy downpour.

He called Bow and said, "I need to meet with you as soon as possible, Bow. I think one of the River City kids ran away from the group while we were taking care of the animals at the Merryweather place."

Bow paused and said, "Okay, buddy, come right in. We'll get on this."

Jacy met with Bow at the sheriff's office, completed some paperwork, and then talked to Bow about ways to locate Django.

"Well, the rain might have slowed him down. But I was thinking that we might want to put Ruby onto his trail. She can find anything," Jacy offered.

"Not a bad idea. Can't hurt," Bow agreed.

Once the rain subsided, Bow and Jacy decided to release Ruby near the Merryweather place. To double their chances, they brought one of Bow's old hounds that was a permanent shelter resident. He might pick up a scent from one of Django's shirts that Jacy had brought along.

After Jacy collected Ruby and loaded Barney the hound, he and Bow rode together in his Jeep. They parked in an area outside of the Merryweather property that was occasionally used as a short cut along a large creek to Greene County. They thought it was the most logical route Django might follow.

Ruby launched into the rainy evening sky, circled overhead, and then swooped down over Jacy's head just to let him know she was checking in. Then she swooped forward, zigzagging back and forth over the path.

At the same time, Bow patted Barney's head and let him nuzzle Django's T-shirt, hoping the hound could locate a similar scent on the trail.

Bow gave Barney a loose leash to let him wander and sniff. He hoped they were not wasting precious time in locating Django, who already had a head start.

Jacy joined Bow and watched Barney get somewhat distracted by a rabbit that shot out from under a bush. Bow asked Jacy why he thought Django had taken off.

"I dunno. I think he is really bored here. He lived with his grandma, Baba Rosa, and had a lot of freedom before she got sick. She taught him about hoodoo medicine and how to make natural remedies and healing teas from herbs. The kid has never been sick a day in his life, at least according to him. He says it's because he wears that acifidity pouch around his neck. Of course, the other kids think it's weird and say it stinks. But they just aren't wise to the ways of the gypsies that roam around the Louisiana bayous," Jacy explained.

"Really? Well, how did he end up here?" Bow asked.

"All I know is what the state's intake report said. Apparently, his grandmother became ill and was put in a nursing home. One of the men, called Johnny Deuce was part of the band of gypsies where his grandmother lived. Supposedly, he was instructed by their leader to take care of Django, or at least feed him. But he was also part of a con game with another guy, Jack Spade, who wrangled invitations to private poker games with some high rollers.

"Together, they worked these poker parties by giving secret signals to one another about their poker hands, and they would end up hauling away some decent cash. That worked out okay for a while until they went to a big game down in Branson. They had to take the kid with them, because they usually were gone for several days at a time to play at these poker games.

"Apparently, there were some bounty boys put on their trail, because of one of their previous con games in Louisiana. They managed to capture the two during one of the big games before they could work their con. The kid was left in their car for a couple of days until the local cops got wise and took him in. Come to find out nobody really could say who was his guardian or parents. And as far as we know, the authorities in Louisiana never could find a birth certificate for him. And so he has been at River City ever since," Jacy explained.

"Sounds like he's had a tough life. It is interesting that he knows about natural healing with herbs and teas. You think Sam might be interested in taking him on as a student? That skill is kind of a lost art, you know," Bow wondered.

"Maybe, but we'll never know if we can't find him," Jacy said.

The rain had stopped. That worried Jacy because it meant Django would be moving farther away.

They walked for another half mile as the evening grew darker. About that time, Ruby zoomed in over Jacy's head and, without landing, started screeching.

Jacy's eyes grew bright with excitement, and he quietly told Bow that he thought Ruby was onto something. Ruby veered off the path to the left and onto a narrow trail that led to a very high, rugged bluff. Both Jacy and Bow hurried quietly toward the area where Ruby was in a holding pattern, circling in the dusky evening sky above.

Jacy motioned for Bow to stay back with Barney, as he proceeded to investigate further. He swiftly and quietly moved through the underbrush to the edge of the bluff. Although the dim light challenged his view, he could see a narrow opening in the side of the bluff that would be perfect shelter from the rain. Slowly, he crept near the opening and detected a slight rustling of movement.

He quietly call out, "Django. No need to be scared. We can work this out."

Django

Slowly, Django emerged from the opening. He started to race back down the hill, only to be stopped in his tracks by Bow.

"No, this is not the way," Bow asserted, as he wrestled him to the ground and then led him back to Jacy. The three walked back to the Jeep with Django hanging his head.

"We can work this out, Django," Jacy said to Django. "We have an idea where you can use your talents to help all living things."

CHAPTER 17

SATURDAY, JUST BEFORE 9 O'CLOCK, Bow arrived at the Merryweather place. Audry was ready to go. She had walked Maggie first thing in the morning and made sure there was plenty of food and water in her bowls in the kitchen. When Bow came to the door, Maggie jumped up and down in excitement and barked at Bow. Apparently, she thought maybe he was going to play with her like he had at the shelter. Bow hugged and talked to her, and she wagged her tail in wild delight. Then he pulled a bag of dog treats out of his pocket and as he gave her one, said, "Good girl!"

Audry petted Maggie on the head, hugged her, and said, "You be a good girl, and I'll bring you more treats later."

Stepping outside, Audry was surprised to see that Bow was driving a classic older lemon yellow muscle car with polished chrome that sparkled in the morning sunlight. Audry said, "Whoa! This is really cool, Bow. This is something my dad would have loved!"

"Thanks! Yes, I restored it myself. It's taken quite a while. Just got the last coat of paint on two weeks ago," he proudly said. Once inside, he started the engine. A strong rumble floated through the air, showing off its power with a big block engine that still had plenty of performance left inside.

As they drove off, Audry thought to herself that it was really quite impressive that Bow had restored this car to its original condition. She had not thought of Bow as a guy who liked fast cars, but as she'd seen so far in Echo Woods, things were not what they appeared to be.

Finally on their way to Springfield, Audry told Bow how happy she was that Maggie was now staying with her. She felt much safer, and Maggie was a fun companion.

Bow

"She lets me know when there is anybody around—even the mailman. She is so smart, and seems to enjoy running with me," Audry proudly said.

Later as they drove along, Audry asked Bow where he was from originally. He told her he was born in Texas, but his family had moved around a lot. His dad and mom were musicians, and they loved playing in roadhouse bands. Finally, they landed in Missouri because his father was also a diesel mechanic. As it turned out, it was the best place for them to settle. There was a big demand for mechanics like his dad to maintain heavy equipment for building roads and large tractors for farming. And, there were plenty of bands where they could sit in and play on the weekends.

"Do you play music like your parents, Bow?" Audry asked.

"Well, I guess you could say that," Bow said with a sheepish smile.

"What about you, Audry?" he asked.

"Oh, I grew up in southern California," she replied. And then she told him about how she had ended up in Missouri.

About 10 miles out of Echo Woods, Bow got a call on his mobile radio. "Lima Charlie Five, do you read me?" the caller asked.

"Roger, this is Lima Charlie Five, what's up?" Bow acknowledged. It was Sam, but he sounded a little more formal than usual.

"Lima Charlie One, here. I was just wondering how the animals are at the Merryweather place," Sam asked.

"10-4 Sam, they are all really happy. Kids from River City are taking care of them. Jacy has everything under control. Glad that it all worked out with Django at your place, Sam," Bow replied.

"Glad to have Django with us now. He's got a lot of knowledge that's been passed onto him. And, we can share with him what we know from the old country," Sam said.

Sam turned serious and said, "Hey, Bow, I just wanted to let you know we heard about another horse theft job out of Taney County today. Chances are they might be headed to the slaughterhouse, like they tried to do the last time. Just wanted to give you a heads up. The trooper said the suspects might be in an old beat up, dark green pickup pulling a stock trailer. It has an expired tag on the back with partial ID of 323. Just hope somebody finds them before they get to the slaughterhouse because you know those guys over at ***that*** slaughterhouse never ask for proper paperwork and will take anything," Sam said with disgust.

"I'll keep that in mind, Sam," Bow replied. "Actually, I'm driving to Springfield with Audry. I'll let you know if I hear anything."

After the radio conversation ended, Audry asked Bow, what does the 'Lima' and 'Charlie' stand for in your radio call?"

"Well, that stands for **L**oral **C**ounty, but how did you know about that?" Bow asked.

"My dad told me about the international alphabet when I was a kid. He thought it was cool for me to know because it was what they used in the military," Audry replied.

"Oh, okay. That's impressive you would remember," Bow said.

"Actually, he taught me a lot a lot of things. I really miss him," Audry revealed.

Bow asked more about her dad's time as a Marine.

Audry told Bow about her dad teaching her self-defense, and how to scuba dive and surf. Bow seemed most interested in the stories she shared from her dad's time in other countries. "He thought peacekeeping was more about war than peace," Audry recalled.

"Well, we have our own wars here in Missouri, unfortunately. Fighting on behalf of animals alone is a huge job, and then trying to keep everybody happy is sometimes impossible," Bow shared.

"Sam said something about the 'old country' on the radio. What did that mean?" Audry asked.

Bow didn't avoid answering the question, but he didn't know quite how to explain that Sam and his kinfolk originated in another part of the world. He told her that Sam's people were from another dimension.

"In the dimension Sam's from, spells and curses could remedy the bad behavior of people and render them harmless. Turning a mean tyrant into a frog usually worked quite well. On the other hand, they could spin up some good energy to combat dark energy and even illnesses," Bow explained. "Allegedly, it was not uncommon in the land where Sam's people had emerged, for some to conjure a spell that could turn people who abused animals into something small and meaningless, where they had no power over much larger animals. Some thought the more powerful sorcerers could actually turn some brutes into animals. They called that a slang name of 'cunja' or other things," Bow said.

"Are you **serious**?!?" Audry skeptically asked.

"I never saw it for myself," Bow admitted but tried to explain it to Audry. "Supposedly that is one reason that Sam and his relatives are very careful about whom they decide to visit or where they go. That's also a main reason they live in remote or hidden locations. It also explains why they mainly work or travel at night."

"No way!" Audry exclaimed with wide eyes. That tale her grandmother had told her about the "little people" deep in the Ozarks maybe, could have been … true, or maybe close to the truth.

Bow thought it would be a good idea to let this settle into Audry's thoughts for a while, because it really was a lot to sort out.

As he turned a knob on the radio, he asked, "Hey, how about some music? Jazz? Oldies? Rock? Blues? Country?"

"I prefer jazz or blues, but it doesn't really matter," Audry replied.

After a while, Audry asked, "So, Bow, one thing I don't understand is, why are there so many animals needing rescue and shelter in Loral County?"

Bow told Audry that the overpopulation at the shelter hadn't always been that way. Apparently, Sam and his people had been rescuing and relocating animals for many, many decades to a lot of different safe havens outside of Loral County.

"But in Loral County it all started when Sam showed up at the shelter. According to him, he was on his way out of town and found a young dog that somebody had dumped along the road near my office. So, he brought the dog to us in hopes it would be returned to its proper owner or could be adopted.

"Since then, Sam and his people have rescued abandoned animals or provided vet services to injured ones. They then bring them to the Loral County shelter or take them to shelters in larger cities. That's primarily a lot of their work. They usually relocate animals during the night when the hoopies are asleep. Sam and his team are masters at picking locks and entering shelters where they leave supplies of food," Bow said.

"And just who are the 'hoopies'?" Audry asked.

"Well, that's a name that Sam and his people call regular people. Humans. Us." Bow explained.

"To help him, I created a type of payment system so that Sam and his family and friends can continue their work. People can pay the shelter for the services that Sam and his people perform, and I make sure Sam gets his money. Or if the hoopies don't have any money, they can bring animal feed, like hay or chow in exchange.

"Then, he recently teamed up with Jacy and his red-tailed hawk, Ruby, who are able to locate animals that have been abandoned or are injured or abused. Those also have been brought to the Loral County shelter or to Sam's place for medical treatment.

"So, the big problem we have faced over the past couple of years is that the county has no money in their budget to buy additional land for a bigger shelter, and certainly no money to build a new facility," Bow explained.

Audry sat in silence, trying to make sense of everything that Bow had just shared. The one thing she knew for sure was that the lack of proper shelter space or care for a growing population of animals was a big problem with no simple answer.

"I really had no idea," Audry said in dazed amazement.

"Yeow, and the problem gets bigger every month," he said.

As they continued down the road, Bow pointed out some of the new restaurants and theaters along the way. Although Audry was interested in seeing wonderful new shopping spots, she remained thoughtful and quiet.

"So, how do you find 'forever homes' for the shelter animals?" Audry finally asked.

"We try to raise awareness by sending pictures and descriptions to various newspapers and weekly shopper publications, but there is no guarantee that they will run. The announcements are published or aired free as a public service, but only if they need filler space or time. We also send those to the local schools and community clubs hoping to attract new people to adopt," Bow explained. "It's really a matter of available space for the homeless animals and time to try and place them."

"What about finding organizations who can sponsor a canine companion for the elderly or people with disabilities?" she asked.

"That's a great idea, but there again we just don't have the money or people power. Some big cities have large facilities and are funded in many ways. They make money from offering obedience classes and doggie daycare services. Others are funded by veterinary services, adoption fees, or wealthy people who have selected them as their favorite charity. They also have access to lots of volunteers from schools and communities.

"Some of the puppies are perfect for training to become security dogs for police departments and the military. And if they are trained to do search and rescue, they can locate missing persons. Just think of the lives that have been saved by the ones who have been trained to sniff out explosive devices. They are excellent service dogs too," Bow said.

"Yes, my dad's friend, K-bar came back from the war in a wheelchair. He had a service dog that was trained to help him open doors, pick up things he had dropped, fetch his newspaper, and retrieve other items for him. That dog was *so* smart, and really was his best friend," Audry recalled.

Bow pulled into a small plaza and said, "Let's get those uniforms and then have some lunch."

Together, Audry and Bow walked into a small shop and an older man greeted Bow. "Bow, good to see ya buddy! Is that a new sidekick you've hired?" the man asked as he smiled at Audry.

Bow smiled and played along with the shopkeeper, "Yeow, I'm thinking about putting her in charge of animal control. She especially likes mules."

Audry couldn't help but smirk at Bow's good-natured teasing.

"This all for you today?" the storekeeper asked as he handed Bow his uniforms on hangers wrapped in a heavy plastic garment bag.

"Yep. That should do it. Thanks a bunch. Just send the bill to the county," Bow replied.

"Stay safe, buddy," the shopkeeper said.

Leaving the shop, Bow told Audry, "The restaurant is close by. Is there any place you want to see before we eat?"

"Not really, but thanks. Actually, I'm hungry," Audry said.

Arriving at Nico's Restaurant, Bow opened the door for Audry. They entered a small alcove with a low curved archway that separated cozy dining sections. A charming young host escorted them to a booth in the back and handed them two menus. Colorful and decorated with original paintings of vineyards and classic bottles of wine, the restaurant featured checked tablecloths and matching napkins. In the background, a sound system played familiar Italian music sung by popular crooners.

The blended aromas of food brought back memories of a restaurant where she and her parents used to eat in "Little Italy" in San Diego.

A beautiful, young, dark-haired waitress brought them a basket of warm freshly baked bread and filled their heavy glasses with ice water. She then asked if they would like a minute before ordering.

"So, Miss Audry, order anything that sounds tempting," Bow offered.

"That is going to be hard to decide," she replied.

"I can assure you that everything is wonderful," Bow said. It was actually his favorite restaurant that he had visited many times. He had become acquainted with the owner, Nico, and his family and could never resist dining there when he visited Springfield.

"They always start us with a small bowl of homemade minestrone soup and Caesar salad," Bow explained.

"Well, I think I will have the spinach and ricotta ravioli in the white sauce," Audry suggested.

"Yes, that is very good. I just can't resist the lasagna though," Bow replied. The waitress returned to the table, and Bow gave her their order. Then shortly a handsome older man approached the table, followed by the young host with a large tray filled with their soups and salads.

"Hey there, Nico. Good to see you, and how are you doing?" Bow stood up and shook the man's hand.

"Great, Bow. Life is good. And it looks like it is being good to you too," he said as he smiled and looked at Audry.

"Oh, this is my friend, Audry Merryweather, Nico."

Audry stood and shook hands with Nico. His hand was strong and warm and she liked him immediately. "It's really a pleasure to meet you," she replied with an engaging smile.

He immediately removed the salads and soup from the large tray and placed them on the table in front of Bow and Audry.

"Now, here you go. Enjoy, and let me know if I need to get a new cook," Nico joked. He then excused himself, and he and the host returned to the front of the restaurant.

Bow grinned and chuckled. "He is so funny. His wife of nearly 30 years is the cook, and there wouldn't probably be a Nico's Restaurant if it weren't for Maria and her family recipes."

After finishing their meal, and before leaving the restaurant, Bow told Nico the food was better than ever. Nico responded with a laugh, "You say that every time, Bow. So, the cook can stay?"

"You are a smart man, Nico, and I think you should take the cook on a vacation and let somebody cook for her—maybe in Italy."

"But how would I make any money?" Nico replied with a laugh and a shrug of his shoulders.

After returning to his car, Bow told Audry, "Nico is quite the joker, but don't be fooled. He and Maria have a lot of financial investments in and around Springfield, and by now they could probably retire. But Maria loves to cook, and Nico is a key member of the business and social community and never meets a stranger. Their restaurant looks like just a nice little Italian restaurant, but really it's more like a community center for families and local civic leaders. If Nico doesn't know what's going on in Springfield, then it probably hasn't or isn't going to happen."

On the way back to Echo Woods, Bow decided to take an older country road that was seldom used but that he loved for its scenery. He had brought his camera and wanted to take some pictures of an old grist mill and the falls that flowed over a dam. This area was a main attraction for fowl that would stop during spring migration for food and water.

Bow stopped on the shoulder of the road near the mill and dam. Stepping out of his car with his camera, he decided to set it in video mode to capture the beautiful flocks that gathered at the dam. Audry joined him and pointed out some especially colorful birds that had settled on the spring grass to feed.

After capturing some nice video of the birds and the falls, Bow and Audry heard an obnoxiously loud roar heading their way, down the hill and toward the mill. They looked up just as a rig and a trailer careened around the old mill's curve.

"Wait!" Bow yelled at Audry. "That's the stock trailer and truck that Sam told me about!"

"Are you sure?" Audry asked with alarm in her voice.

"Well, yeow!" Bow yelled emphatically. "It's an old dark green pickup pulling a junky stock trailer!

"Get in the car!" he yelled.

He was already in the car with the engine roaring, when Audry jumped in. He peeled out off the shoulder and sped down the road trying to locate the stock trailer and truck.

Shortly, they caught up with the rig, and Bow decided to radio the Missouri Highway Patrol.

He dialed his radio into a private setting, clicked the switch and announced, "Breaker MHP 100, come in. This is Lima Charlie Five, Bow Holiday. I think I have sighted the old truck and trailer that was reported this morning regarding the Taney County horse theft. I'm located south of the old Powers' grist mill on county road double Z. I'm following."

Audry double-checked her seat belt and searched the horizon for a sighting of the rig, while Bow floored the gas pedal and headed down the road.

Within a minute, Audry yelled, "There!" and pointed to the stock trailer that had rounded a curve ahead.

"Okay, we can follow and hope that the patrol have their ears on … and show up!" Bow said with worry. "I'm out of my territory and really can't do anything as a deputy here."

The driver and passenger of the pickup must have been spooked by the yellow car that kept following them. They sped up and began to drive erratically. Although Bow had slowed his pursuit, he kept a steady tail on the truck.

"That's the tag, all right! Expired, and last three numbers are 323," Bow asserted.

The truck now topped a hill that would descend into a valley below. The road was dangerously narrow at this point, with no shoulders and deep ditches on both sides. The old hills and pot-holed roads in this location were unforgiving of modern vehicles and were better suited for horses or off-road vehicles.

Suddenly, the old truck jerked to the right and pitched with the trailer off the road into a shallow valley.

Bow yelled, "Oh *no*! That old truck must have blown a tire. We have got to go see if we can help. Those animals in the stock trailer have got to be terrified, if not injured!"

Bow immediately stopped the car, and both he and Audry jumped out and ran to the accident scene.

Shock filled their faces as they looked down on the wreckage from the road and heard the horses, screaming with fright. The trailer was lying on its side, and two men had been thrown from the truck and lay not moving on the ground nearby. The truck would never roll again.

In high alert mode, Bow told Audry, "Okay, I'm going to call some people I know that can help me get the animals out of the trailer. Then I'll check on the occupants and after that, I'm going back to the trailer and try to calm the animals. I need for you to call Sam and get some of his people here, including Django!"

Audry got back in the car after Bow called the large-animal rescue service, and called Sam on the radio and as Bow had instructed.

94

But, she was not entirely sure of what the men would do once they became conscious if they were not, in fact, dead. She looked around in Bow's car for any kind of gear that could be used to restrain them if necessary. Not finding anything, she pulled the lever on the trunk, did a quick search and found it empty. Finally she looked in the glove box to see if there was something there.

Not surprising, but still a clear indication of Bow's world, she found a revolver and handcuffs. She grabbed them, stuck them in her jean jacket pockets and ran back to the scene.

She saw Bow, working feverishly with a tire iron from his trunk to pry open the stock trailer to at least allow the animals their freedom. He knew that the type of shock they had experienced could prove fatal.

As Audry scaled down the incline, one of the men began to stir and the other one was already on his knees trying to get his bearings and stand up.

The Marine's daughter suddenly mustered the courage that she had learned from her father and took full command of the situation. Boldly Audry barked, "Hold it right there! Don't even think about moving!"

One of the men was groggy, banged up with cuts and bruises on his head, but he defiantly asked, "Oh, yeow, and what are **YOU** gonna do about it?"

She pulled the gun from her pocket and responded, "Don't move, or you'll wish you hadn't!"

The other man slowly started to crawl away. To prove her point, Audry fired a shot over his head. The sound immediately grounded him again. He lay prone on the ground and began to whine and cry. "Don't shoot me, don't shoot me, don't shoot me! It wasn't my idea!" he wailed.

It wasn't long until a beefy transport truck pulling a self-contained trailer arrived. Bow had worked with this team in the past and watched them expertly begin to remove two horses and a young colt from the wrecked trailer. One of the horses had lacerations and needed immediate attention.

Bow instructed the men to take the horses to the shelter.

Immediately, Audry interrupted Bow, and insisted that they be transported to her property, where they could be treated and recover in her stable.

As Audry turned to get back in Bow's car to collect her thoughts, Sam appeared from nowhere next to her and asked, "Are you okay?"

Startled and perplexed, Audry asked, "Well, am I? Sometimes, I don't think I know if I am, or if I am not even here."

"Oh, yes, you are just fine. Actually, Django and the others will be meeting the rescue unit at your place," Sam assured Audry.

About that time, the local authorities arrived and hauled off the suspected horse thieves. One was heard yelling, while pointing at Audry, "Arrest her! She could have kilt me!"

Back at the Merryweather property, Django, Izzy, Santos, and several others from Sam's community sat back and watched the rescue team unload the horses and deliver them into the stable. One older mare had lacerations from the wreck and needed immediate attention. The team's vet had given her a mild tranquilizer and administered some first aid. The others simply needed to be fed and watered.

Izzy spoke quietly to Django, "So, do you need our help, or can we just watch you?" Django said, "It is all good. We are all good. Thank you."

Then without another word, he removed a leather bag from an old burlap knapsack that he carried over his shoulder. From this he took out a small round metal canister, followed by a narrow handmade pottery tray. He then withdrew a wooden match from a small roll of brown paper, and finally extracted a long eagle's feather.

He opened the canister, released a mound of mixed herbs onto the tray, struck a match on an old stable wall board, and lit the mixture until it briefly burned bright orange. Soon it died down and released a healthy column of smoke. Django held the eagle's feather by its spine and began gently waving it over the smoke to circulate over and around the mare.

Django then asked Izzy, "Did you bring Miss Vernie's liniment?"

Izzy replied, "Yes, and it is some of her best."

Django approached the mare, which was lying on a huge bed of straw. He calmly hummed and withdrew a small hand bell from his jacket pocket. He rang it slowly around the stable. It emitted a low calming sound, and this was accompanied by a soothing verse he said repeatedly, "Healing now, healing forever. Healing now, healing forever."

From his jacket's breast pocket, Django withdrew a small whittled reed whistle that had been sized to blow a perfect B flat tone. It was like a natural pitch pipe. He lightly blew on the whistle, matched the tone with his voice, and repeated a centuries-old murmur in the monotone that matched the whistle note.

"Round, round, and round!
Be thou, be thou very sound.
The devil shall not come to thee,
God, God shall be with thee!
Sweet God drive away
From the horse's body
The Core of Evil!
Be beautiful! Be divine! Be complete!
Be frolicsome and good.
Seven spirits hear!
Protect this animal
Ever, and forever!"

Django placed his hands on the mare and calmly hummed to her. Then he gently massaged Miss Vernie's liniment onto her bruises and wounds.

The mare was amazingly calm, and in the corner of the stable, Sam could be seen smiling. He knew that everything would truly be, as Django had said, "All good."

CHAPTER 18

AUDRY HAD RECOVERED FROM HER trip with Bow and was actually looking forward to future trips to Springfield, and especially to Nico's—but without any chaos or drama!

She thought Bow was really a nice person and would make a good friend. She had not met many people in Echo Woods, except for Sam and his associates. And she had to admit, they all were nice, but Bow was actually a hoopie and was closer to her age. They seemed to enjoy some of the same things—bookstores, Italian food, and jazz, just to name a few. Oh, and like him, she liked animals. He was easy to talk to and had many friends.

The following Monday, as Audry was getting ready to go back to her office to pick up new assignments, she remembered she hadn't checked her mailbox after a very eventful weekend. She flipped open the box and among the junk mail was a letter from Beryl and Benz, LLC, in St. Louis. Once she opened it, she saw it was a letter from a law firm requesting that she call them at her earliest convenience.

Admittedly she was a bit disturbed. She called the number listed in the letter.

The voice on the other end said, "Beryl and Benz, may I help you?"

"Yes, my name is Audry Merryweather and I am calling regarding a letter I received from your firm. It requested that I contact a Ms. Fitzgerald with your office," Audry said.

"Please hold, and I will get back with you in just a moment," the receptionist replied.

Audry was perplexed and concerned. She couldn't imagine why a law firm was contacting her.

Soon the woman was back on the line and said, "Miss Merryweather, attorney Fitzgerald, with our firm needs to meet with you in person. It is regarding some unfinished business regarding your late father. We had a difficult time locating your new address, and we're glad we can get this matter completed."

"Oh, dear," Audry said, somewhat disturbed.

"Oh, it is nothing that should concern you, but we will need to see you in person here in St. Louis, and you need to bring a current photo ID," the assistant instructed.

"Well, okay, that's fine. When should I plan to be there?" Audry asked.

"Well, Ms. Fitzgerald said she is available on Wednesday at 1 p.m. to speak with you. Will that work for you, Miss Merryweather?" asked the woman.

"Yes, I can arrange that," Audry replied.

"Very good. We are located in downtown St. Louis at the address that appears in your letter," the woman instructed.

After saying goodbye, Audry hung up the phone and immediately wondered what on earth this legal matter was all about! Her dad and uncle certainly would find Echo Woods **anything** but boring these days. And lately, it would have probably been too much for even them.

Audry drove to the legal aid office where she worked and spoke to her boss, Mary. Although they had talked about work on the phone during her time off, she hadn't seen her in a while.

"Hi Audry, it is good to see you! How are you?" Mary asked.

"Good to see you too, Mary. I've been busier than I thought, getting the old place shaped up," Audry replied. "I've come to pick up some files and check on my schedule. Anything out of the ordinary going on here?" Audry asked.

"Not really, just a couple of roughnecks wanting some legal representation. They claim somebody stole their mule," Mary said.

Audry silently gulped and her eyes grew larger.

Mary looked at her strangely and said, "You okay, Audry?"

"Oh, yes, just a bit, uh, uh, surprised. Mules. Very odd," Audry eventually replied.

"We talked to Deputy Holiday to obtain any reports of a stolen mule, and he said there weren't any. Anyway, we declined, because our attorneys are booked up right now," Mary explained.

Audry's heart was beating rapidly, and she hurriedly collected files and checked her mailbox. On the way out of the office, Audry said to Mary, "See you next week. I'll email or fax the next documents back to you before then."

Audry was indeed flustered. Ohfercryinoutloud! She could **not** believe what she had just heard. A mule theft? It **must** have been the Bitler brothers. She decided right then and there that she was going to take Maggie and go tomorrow to St. Louis just to get away from all of the stress of Echo Woods. She immediately got on the phone when she got home, booked a hotel that accepted pets, and began to pack for the trip. At the same time, Maggie started whining and wandering from room to room.

Audry stooped down to pet Maggie and reassured her that everything was fine. They were just going "bye-bye" on a little trip. Apparently Maggie could understand something of the human language, because she calmed down.

First thing on Tuesday morning, Audry locked up the house, loaded her SUV, activated her GPS, and headed northeast **out of town**.

Maggie was a great traveling companion and kept busy looking at the scenery. They stopped after a couple of hours at a roadside park. Audry gave Maggie fresh water in her travel dish and let her walk and take a potty break.

Later, Audry arrived at the hotel not far from the river in St. Charles. It was a beautiful historical town outside of St. Louis, and a place her mother enjoyed visiting and drawing. In the summer months, musicians performed in the park on the bandstand. Quaint restaurants and shops lined the brick-paved streets, and the sounds of the rushing river could be heard nearby.

Audry hooked the leash to Maggie's collar and walked with her to the front desk of the hotel. Several people admired Maggie's sweet face and pretty coat. Two small girls giggled with delight at the sight of Maggie and asked if they could pet her.

Audry agreed, and Maggie greeted them with a wagging tail and a wiggle of her butt. Audry thanked the clerk for her key and grabbed a cart on her way out of the office. Together they loaded Audry's suitcase and laptop, Maggie's bed, and some food for both of them onto the cart.

Once the cart was unloaded in her room, Audry kicked off her shoes, changed into her PJs, found an interesting movie on the television, and browsed through a new magazine. Maggie looked at her, as Audry said, "Maggie, sometimes girls have to do what girls have to do. We go on vacation or find a good movie."

Audry was up at about 7:30 on Wednesday morning when Maggie nuzzled her face with her nose letting her know she needed to go outside. Audry jumped up, put on her sweats, and took Maggie for a short walk. The morning river air smelled musky, but the temperature was perfect.

After returning, Audry wrote a couple of letters and emailed some completed documents back to the legal aid office. She made sure Maggie had fresh food and water, changed clothes, and then left for her appointment at the attorney's office.

The change of scenery was very pleasant, and Audry decided to stay a couple more days and head back to Echo Woods on Friday. She heard there was a special exhibit at the St. Louis Art Museum that she wanted to see, and she absolutely did not want to miss one of her favorite Broadway plays at the grand old historical theater downtown. Those were both "must-see" events that she could not catch in Echo Woods.

Audry found the law firm and parked in a nearby public garage. She had tried to guess about possible reasons the firm had scheduled this meeting with her, but she was still mystified. She took the elevator to the fourth floor, found the proper suite number, and then entered. She told the receptionist her name and that she had an appointment with attorney Fitzgerald.

"Yes, Miss Merryweather, we've been expecting you and she will be right with you," the receptionist informed her. She took a seat near a window and looked out at the bustling city. It certainly seemed noisier than she remembered. But maybe it was because she had become used to the quiet of Echo Woods. Signs advertising the major league baseball games could be seen everywhere. And in the distance she could hear a tugboat horn.

A woman in a stylish gray, tweed suit entered the waiting area and addressed her, "Miss Merryweather? I'm attorney Fitzgerald. I really appreciate you traveling here today to meet with us. Would you like to follow me to my office?"

Audry thought she was awfully formal. But then again, city manners, and especially those in a law firm, are really different from the casual day-to-day culture of Echo Woods.

"Yes, thank you," Audry responded. Audry followed Ms. Fitzgerald to her office and took a seat as Ms. Fitzgerald suggested.

"Miss Merryweather, I was so sorry to hear of your father's passing, and the reason we needed to meet with you is to settle a final transaction of his will. You see, your father was involved in a very high-risk occupation that paid very well. He also wanted to make sure that if anything ever happened to him, you would have no money worries. As a result, he had set up an investment program that would be paid in full upon an accidental death.

"And that is the reason for our meeting. We need to pay out that benefit to you, and wanted to give you the names of some trusted firms that can provide sound advice for money management. These are highly respected advisors and can guide you or answer any questions you may have," the attorney explained.

"Well, I never knew anything about this," Audry slowly replied.

"That is understandable and typical," Ms. Fitzgerald assured her.

"But, how much exactly is this inheritance?" Audry asked faintly.

"It is in the amount of five point one million dollars, Miss Merryweather," the attorney quietly said.

"Ex-cuse me???" Audry choked in disbelief.

"Your benefit is five point one million dollars," the attorney said again.

"There must be some mistake. Are you sure about this? I mean that is a **LOT** of money!"

"Precisely, Miss Merryweather," Ms. Fitzgerald responded. "Would you like for me to make some phone calls while you are in town and see if any of the investment counselors can meet with you while you are in St. Louis?"

"Uh, well, oh, geez, that probably would be a really good idea," she said, flustered by this sudden news.

"Very well then. First I need to see some identification and have you sign some papers. In the meantime, I'll have my assistant make some phone calls. How long will you be in town?" Ms. Fitzgerald asked.

Audry showed the attorney her passport for identification and then weakly responded, "Through Friday."

Ms. Fitzgerald placed a call and said, "Tina, can you see if one of the investment firms on our referral list can see Miss Merryweather tomorrow or Friday, and then set it up?"

After she hung up, she presented several documents for Audry to read and sign, and requested routing and account numbers for Audry's bank savings account for an electronic transfer of the funds in the amount of $5,100,000 to her bank in Springfield.

Audry stared at the transaction document in disbelief. She could feel herself getting flushed and slightly nauseous.

"Miss Merryweather? Can I get you some water? You don't look very well," Miss Fitzgerald said.

Soon her phone rang, and she wrote information on a small pad. She then said to Audry, "Miss Merryweather, we have arranged for you to meet with a firm on Friday morning at 10 a.m."

As the attorney handed her a note she continued, "Here is the person you will be meeting with and her address. It is not far from this location, so it should be easy for you to find."

"Do you have any questions Miss Merryweather?" she asked. "If you don't then I will walk you out, but you can always call me in the future if you do. Here's my card."

Ms. Fitzgerald shook Audry's hand and wished her good luck with her future plans and safe travels back to Echo Woods.

CHAPTER 19

AUDRY MET WITH THE FINANCIAL advisor and agreed to proceed with her suggestions. The funds would be initially deposited in her savings account at her bank in Springfield and she could meet with and advise her banker of her money management plans.

Driving back to Echo Woods, Audry was deep in thought and barely noticed scenery that usually would have attracted her attention. She thought about all the possible plans that could be developed and how they would benefit herself and others. Her brain was whirling with ideas, and she found it hard to concentrate on the road and not to speed.

Meanwhile, back in Echo Woods, routine daily activities had come to a screeching halt. First of all, the adoption day for the shelter animals had come and gone. That was because Audry's barn door had accidently been left open at feeding time one morning, and a couple of the dogs got out. They eventually came back, and were put back in the barn for safe keeping. But the adoptive families were contacted and told there would be a slight delay in the scheduled day for pick up and adoption.

That created a chain reaction, because Bow tried several times to phone Audry to tell her about the delay but couldn't reach her. He was disturbed because Audry hadn't mentioned she was going to be gone. He had left two messages on her answering machine to call him, but she hadn't. He also did not have her cell phone number, because cell phones did not work very well in Echo Woods. That was the reason many people used land mobile radio systems. Most Echo Woods people carried cell phones only when traveling out of the area.

Then, he thought, was she just not answering the phone because it was him? Was she avoiding him? Had the misadventure and chaos of Saturday been too much? He thought about their conversations, but nothing seemed to stick out in his mind as offensive.

To make matters worse, Sam had brought several more rescued animals to the shelter. The new additions were two sheep and a baby goat that needed to be bottle fed. Then when Bow tried to contact Jacy on the radio, Jacy didn't respond. He thought Jacy might have seen Audry when he and the kids had fed the animals that morning. He also wanted to make sure that all of the animals were doing okay.

By noon Thursday, Bow decided to drive out to Audry's place and see if there was anything amiss. He hooked up a small transport trailer to one of the county pickups, loaded and secured the sheep in the back, and headed to Audry's place. There he planned to leave the sheep with the rest of the animals and also to leave a note for Jacy to call him.

After putting the sheep in the barn, he looked around and saw that the barn was clean, with plenty of water and food for the animals. He put out a bin of feed for the sheep and then secured the barn door behind him.

Fortunately, the horses in the stable were recovering quite well and would be picked up by their real owners next week. Even the old mare had made a remarkable recovery. She enjoyed the special attention that the River City kids gave her, especially the apples they brought her daily.

He saw Stella in the barn lot munching on tender grass. She seemed quite content but bellowed at him, walked to the gate, and expected to be petted on the head. The cats in the workshop were either playing or napping, and everything seemed in order. Jacy and his crew had done a fine job of caring for the shelter animals.

Before getting into the pickup, he went to Audry's back porch and knocked on the door. Like the phone calls he had made, there was no answer. He looked around and saw that nothing was out of place, except that her SUV was gone. And since Maggie hadn't barked when he knocked on the door, he figured Audry must have taken Maggie with her.

Bow admitted to himself he really didn't know what was going on. She hadn't decided to move, had she? He knew that Echo Woods was very different from places she had lived before and that, since her move, she had faced a lot of unusual events. First of all, there was Sam's appearance, then animal rescues, the Bitler brothers' invasion, and her property being used to shelter animals, the horse thieves on the run….

Well, maybe she had decided it was all too much. He guessed that altogether the events seemed a bit much to face in a short period of time. Bow guessed maybe Audry was really more of a city girl. She was different—pretty and nice too, and very independent. But she seemed to truly enjoy the time when Sam had shown her the improvements made to the property and even to enjoy the animals.

Bow finally decided to quit debating with himself over Audry, and where she was, and why. He told himself he was just wasting time fretting about Audry, and he finally decided to go back to the shelter and take care of all of his chores.

When he got back to the office, it was time to feed the baby goat. Again. So small, but bright-eyed and spunky. That was good to see. This kid goat would be just fine. He fixed her bottle. At first she was hesitant, but once she got a taste of the formula in the bottle, there was no stopping her from eating. He was chuckling to himself when Sam appeared.

"Hey Sam, look at this little girl," Bow said.

Sam admired the baby goat and asked, "What do you want to name her, Bow?"

"How about Sunny, since she seems so bright and cheerful?" Bow asked.

Sam agreed that it would make a good name, and then he asked about when the animals at Audry's place were going to meet their new owners. Sam noticed a puzzled but sad look come over Bow's face.

"Well, I don't exactly know," Bow slowly replied. "We really need to have Audry's permission for people to be picking up their animals from her property."

"So, is that a problem?" Sam asked.

"Well, it might be, because Audry's, well, gone," Bow quietly replied.

"Gone? Like in, gone for a little while, or gone for good?" Sam asked with a very peculiar look on his face.

"I don't know," Bow replied gloomily.

"Well, Bow, you look a little glum about that," Sam said with a raised eyebrow.

"Well, she certainly *is* a special kind of person. I've not met anybody quite like her before, and we went to Springfield Saturday and had a very nice time, until everything went haywire," Bow said, notably annoyed.

"It'll be okay. I'll have some of my people see if they can find her," Sam reassured Bow.

Early Friday evening, Audry arrived back home. She had plenty of time to ponder everything from her meetings in St. Louis, and she had decided that the Merryweather property needed a new life that included the old fairgrounds that she now owned.

Before taking a run with Maggie down the road, she checked her answering machine and saw that there were several messages. One was from her work, one was from an old friend in California, and two were from Bow.

In the two from Bow, he sounded concerned. In the first message, he wondered if she was okay, because he hadn't been able to reach her to set up a new time for the adoptive owners to pick up their animals. In the second message, he asked again if she was okay and to call him and let him know when she got the message.

She wasn't quite ready to talk to anybody right now, because her mind was still swirling with everything that had happened over the last week. To collect her thoughts, Audry fed and watered Maggie and was brushing the dog's coat when there was a knock on her back door. Maggie barked a little but then started wagging her tail.

Audry opened the door, and there stood Sam. "Hi ho," he said.

"Hi Sam, how are you?" she asked.

"Good, good, but you need to call Bow and let him know you are okay," Sam immediately instructed.

"Oh, really?" she said, surprised.

"Well, yes, the boy is a bit concerned," Sam replied. "I knew you were okay, but it really wasn't my place to tell him that. Ruby had you spotted on your way back from St. Louis," Sam revealed.

"Ru-by?" Audry questioned, as her voice rose.

"Yes, Ruby is Jacy's very smart red-tailed hawk. There are some very clever animals among us that are aware of all of the activities of the hoopies."

"Wow! I didn't mean to worry people. I had no idea anybody really cared. Besides, I just got home. Actually, you were on my mind, Sam, most of the way home," Audry said. And with that, Audry poured out the story about why she had to suddenly go out of town.

And, then she asked, "Sam, what does your construction schedule look like for the upcoming months?"

With that question, Audry opened the door to a whole new chapter in Echo Woods history, even though it would take a while to see the results.

CHAPTER 20

SAM AND AUDRY AGREED THAT they would meet again at the first of the week to lay out the plans and construction for what Audry referred to as the Preserve. Audry had told Sam most of the story about how this occurred, but she asked him to promise that for now, it would only be known as a special arrangement with a newly formed non-profit group out of St. Louis. Audry said she wanted people to think of her as only the special events director with this non-profit, and nothing more. At the end of Audry's story, Sam was unusually quiet and thoughtful.

Finally, Audry asked if he was okay. Sam replied, "Oh, yes. I really am not surprised, though. You come from a long line of humanitarians and people that believed in honoring one another—animals included.

"There was a very wise person who actually named this area when it was originally founded, based upon his philosophy. He said that what you give, you get, and that life is like an echo. What you send out, comes back. That is why this area is called Echo Woods—in the hopes that all people who live here will send out goodness," Sam explained. "I can see that you have brought that back home, Audry."

After Sam left, Audry thought a long time about what he had said. He obviously was very wise, and she knew that she could count on him to help make her dream of the new Merryweather property come true.

As she heard the alert beep on her answering machine, it reminded her that she really needed to return Bow's call. She punched in the numbers on the phone, and after three rings Bow answered, "Hello?"

Merryweather Homestead

"Well, hello Deputy Holliday, I guess I owe you a phone call," Audry said in a cheery voice.

"I should say you do, Miss Merryweather. Are you okay?" Bow asked as a big smile spread across his face. "We have been a bit worried about you, since you didn't tell anybody you were going out of town."

"Oh, that can't be," she teased. "Well, I had to make a quick trip out of town to take care of some of my dad's old business in St. Louis. Did I miss anything exciting here?"

"Well, I don't recall anything exceptional, but you have two new sheep in your barn, and there is a baby goat here at the shelter. She is so funny, but still has to be bottle fed. She jumps stiff-legged, straight up in the air! Her name is Sunny," Bow told her, chuckling.

"She sounds delightful. I'd like to see her," Audry said.

"How about if I bring her by tomorrow afternoon and maybe we can catch up?" Bow asked.

"Well, sure," Audry replied with a smile on her face. "What time?"

"Oh, I was thinking about 1 o'clock. Will that work for you?" he asked.

"Sure, I'll see you then, okay?" she responded.

"You bet!" Bow said as he hung up.

Audry finished brushing Maggie and said to her, "You are such a pretty girl, and so smart. And, Bow is coming to see us tomorrow!"

Maggie looked at Audry and wiggled her butt and wagged her tail at the same time. Audry gave her a big hug and then started writing and sketching images on a large sheet of graph paper of the project that she and Sam would be discussing on Monday.

Bow arrived the next day and was excited for Audry to see Sunny. He had put a very small harness on her and attached a long leash. He tried to lead the tiny goat to Audry's back door. She certainly had a mind of her own, and he was glad she was attached to a leash because she was trying to take off in many directions to explore. It was funny to see Bow try to wrangle a very small but lively goat.

Audry said, "Hey, there, I have never seen anybody try to walk a goat before!"

"Hi, I'd like to see you manage her. She is a wild one," Bow chuckled.

Audry walked out with Maggie. As soon as Sunny saw Maggie, she jumped straight up in the air and then lowered her head and stared at Maggie. Maggie wagged her tail and looked at Sunny with her ears cocked forward showing her curiosity about this small but fiery animal.

"She is adorable, Bow," Audry said. "Let's walk her out to the dog pens and let her play for a while."

Bow, leading Sunny, walked with Audry and Maggie behind the old workshop and let Sunny loose inside the fenced area. She kicked and butted an old plastic bucket that had been left behind. As they watched Sunny play, Audry and Bow sat on a fence railing and talked about her trip out of town and her visits to the museum and other sights around St. Charles.

"Oh, that is a beautiful place," Bow said. "I love St. Charles."

After about an hour, Bow told Audry he should be getting Sunny back to the shelter. He asked if she wanted to ride along and then maybe grab some pizza at Franco's Cafe. After all, it was Saturday and that was the dish of the day on the weekend. "Mrs. Franco knows the teenagers love her pizza," Bow said.

As Audry and Bow headed back to the house, several little people riding small mules appeared on the scene near the barn.

Audry blinked her eyes to make sure she was seeing what she thought she was seeing. Bow smiled and waved hello to the visitors.

"Hi Jerzy, how's it going?" Bow asked the taller rider in the group.

"We're mighty fine today, Bow," Jerzy replied. "Glad to see you're back, Miss Audry."

"Why, uh, I, um, thank you. Had no idea I was missed," Audry stammered.

Jerzy then tipped his hunting hat toward Audry, as he and his two companions rode their mules back toward Echo Woods.

"Bow, who are those people?" Audry asked with a very peculiar look on her face.

"Well, those are some of Sam's trusted relatives," Bow explained. "They helped settle Echo Woods decades ago."

"*Decades* ago?" Audry asked.

"Yeow, you see, Sam and his kinfolk don't age quite like we do," Bow replied. "They were actually in these parts well before your house was built. They help Sam with all kinds of odd jobs, maintaining history books that tell the real truth of Echo Woods and Loral County, and family trees for hoopies and animals. They also help Sam's people keep records of remedies that help heal all of the animals they treat. Oh, and they help to update the records for cemeteries."

"You're serious?!" Audry asked as her voice rose.

"Well, yes, but it's not something we talk about with other hoopies that probably would never truly understand the real Echo Woods," Bow explained.

"Oh, I see that, because *I* barely understand the real Echo Woods!" Audry said in frustration.

"It's all good, Audry," Bow quietly reassured her. "Just think of it as a way of life, but that some of it is, you might say, 'enchanted.' And, I should let you know that they don't allow just anybody to actually see them. So you should consider yourself to be very special, Audry."

"I guess that should make me feel good, but I really don't understand," Audry replied.

"It is what it is," Bow assured her. "Nothing to worry about. Now, how about let's take Sunny to the shelter and then get some pizza, before Mrs. Franco runs out?"

CHAPTER 21

ON THE FOLLOWING MONDAY MORNING, Sam showed up at Audry's with his backpack overflowing. Long paper rolls, yellowed with age, stuck out of Sam's bag. He also carried a large pad, and a couple of pencils stuck out of one of his small pockets.

Audry had set the table for tea, and she opened the door before Sam could knock.

"Hi ho, and good morning!" Sam greeted Audry.

"Come on in, Sam," Audry invited. "I have so many ideas, and I can't stop thinking about the possibilities!"

Shortly, Sam had his large pad on Audry's kitchen table, drawing out sketches as Audry shared her vision of the new Loral County Preserve. A haven for humans and animals alike, it would also be powered with the latest in wind and solar energy. First on Sam's drawing pad appeared a series of solar panels and wind turbines that would border all of the Merryweather land. New buildings would include solar panels, but she insisted that the barn, house, and older buildings remain in their original state.

Sam drew effortlessly, as if he could read Audry's mind. A new cultural arts conservatory would take center stage between the homestead and the new fairgrounds. Its retractable roof would allow summer evenings under the stars for concerts, plays, and live performances by popular entertainers and even those who simply wanted to view the constellations and shooting stars.

Throughout the rest of the year, the roof would be closed and the amphitheater would serve as a complex for classes, speakers, talent shows, dance and gymnastic competitions, art exhibits, and many other cultural arts events for all residents, far and wide, to enjoy.

Merryweather Barn

To further encourage the development of visual arts, Audry had included several, round, glass-topped, dome pods. These would be constructed of natural materials, including recycled glass, and placed in harmony with the natural habitat. With plenty of natural lighting, artists and writers could have the perfect location where they could quietly work on their projects. Even musicians would find the pods useful for individual practice time.

In the finished estate, photographers and birdwatchers would also have access to tall observation towers in the timber area.

As for the wide range of animals that needed forever homes, which was Audry's main focus, she asked Sam just how many accommodations would be needed to properly care for them.

"That is a never ending project, Audry. But, with the right kind of building, they could be available for viewing all the time," Sam advised. "A petting zoo would certainly attract more visitors, and that could create some income for you."

"Students and others can volunteer valuable time and learn how to care for animals as part of educational programs," Audry suggested.

"Yes, and with the new animal hospital that you have proposed, your non-profit can earn money from their treatment and care," Sam said. "It can offer routine vaccinations and other services that are now done only in Springfield."

The landscape surrounding the property would be planted in corn that could not only feed many rescued animals but also serve as a giant corn maze for visitors to the newly revived Loral County Fair in the fall.

When Audry begin talking about her childhood memories of the fairgrounds, buildings, and the carnival rides, Sam interrupted her and asked, "Audry, I think I have an idea of what you mean."

He then withdrew the old long, yellowed rolls from his backpack. He unfolded them and carefully laid them out flat on Audry's kitchen table. The faded ink drawings and labels showed a layout of stables, corrals, and show barns, scattered around a large open area with a large sign with bold lettering read "AMUSEMENTS."

"That is amazing, Sam!" Audry exclaimed. "How did you know?!"

"My people built the original fairgrounds," Sam quietly admitted.

CHAPTER 22

SAM AGREED TO FINISH UP additional layouts and show them to Audry the following week. However, before any construction could begin, Audry needed to travel to Springfield and open a special account with her bank as the financial counselor in St. Louis had advised.

On Wednesday, Audry gathered her paperwork, loaded Maggie in her SUV, and headed to Springfield. She had been given the name of the officer with her bank who could help manage her special account. She had to admit she was a bit nervous. This was a huge project she was undertaking, but she trusted her advisor in St. Louis, and she especially had confidence in Sam and his people to create the new Loral County Preserve and Fairgrounds.

The drive to Springfield was uneventful, and the spring air was so refreshing. She noticed that the redbud and dogwood trees were flowering. With the bright green grass and bushes, it was an artist's wonderland for painting beautiful landscapes.

Audry arrived at First Bank of Greene County, gathered her portfolio of papers, and walked Maggie into the bank. At the customer service desk, she asked to speak to the special accounts officer. Soon a tall, middle-aged woman escorted her to her desk and introduced herself as Sheila Baxter.

After reviewing Audry's paperwork, Ms. Baxter recognized her name, and said, "We have been expecting you, Miss Merryweather, and I'm glad you and your friend could visit us today. And, may I ask your friend's name?"

"Oh, why of course. This is Maggie," Audry said as she nodded to Maggie.

The bank officer politely asked Audry if her friend would like a small treat, all-natural of course.

"Oh, sure. And, you have made a new friend for life," Audry said and smiled.

"Now, Miss Merryweather, it will take a few minutes to draft our paperwork to set up your special account. Can I get you some coffee, tea, or water?" she asked.

"Water is fine, Ms. Baxter, and thank you," Audry responded.

"Good, good. I'll bring it to you in our private lounge where you can relax while I complete your paperwork for signature," Ms. Baxter replied.

As Audry entered the lounge area with overstuffed couches, chairs, a television and books, a man's voice from behind her said, "Well, it is nice to see you again."

Turning around she saw it was, Nico, the man who owned the Italian restaurant where she and Bow had eaten.

She smiled, and said, "Well, it is very nice to see you too, Nico."

"And you have a lovely dog. I see. But, where is that young man? Bow?"

She blushed slightly, laughed, and said, "He is probably keeping everybody happy around Echo Woods."

"Please tell him hello for Maria and me. You two need to stop in again real soon. Maria has come up with a new dessert. You'll have to try it," Nico said. "As a matter of fact, dinner for you two, the next time you visit, is on me. No, take that back, it's on Maria!" Nico said as he gave a hearty chuckle.

"That is so nice of you, Nico. Thank you so much! We'll look forward to that!" Audry said with sincere appreciation and extended her hand to shake his. He gripped her hand, patted her back with the other, and said, "Okay, see you soon!"

Audry wondered how in the world she had happened to run into Nico at the bank. Well, Bow did say Nico was very involved in the business community, so that would explain why he would be at the bank. How was she going to explain this to Bow if she took him to dinner? She wouldn't tell Bow she had been to the bank. That was something she would just simply have to think about later. But right now, she needed to get her account set up, so Sam could start construction.

Shortly thereafter, Ms. Baxter appeared and asked Audry to join her in her office. After Ms. Baxter explained the details of the account, Audry signed the paperwork with the bank. And, with the final stroke of the pen, the Loral County Preserve and Fairgrounds was born.

CHAPTER 23

ONCE ON THE HIGHWAY BACK to Loral County, Audry could finally relax. The last couple of weeks had been filled with mind-spinning surprises. She had never imagined that she would someday be discreetly leading a foundation that would not only benefit animals, but also foster cultural art development for humans.

She was about halfway home on the highway, when she noticed a large new billboard along the road. It caught her eye immediately because **ECHO WOODS** appeared in huge yellow letters. Glancing further, while trying to drive, she read, "Coming Soon! The all new, **LORAL COUNTY PRESERVE AND FAIRGROUNDS**."

WHAT!?!?!?!?! Stomping on the brake, she almost skidded her SUV into the ditch. After regaining control, she carefully slowed to a stop on the shoulder and turned on her emergency blinkers. She slowly backed up so that she could carefully reread the billboard. Surely there had been some mistake! But plain as day, the sign also said, **"Petting Zoo—Animal Adoption Center—Carnival Rides—Seven Sisters Smorgy—Family Fun for Everyone"**

No, she had not imagined it. How could this be, and how could it happen so quickly?!? She knew the answer, even before asking herself the question. Sam. Such a simple name for somebody who always created more mystery than answers. It seemed his ideas ended up with more chaos than peace! At least for Audry ….

Audry fumed and said out loud, "Sam and his BIG ideas!"

Collecting herself, Audry slowly pulled back on the highway. She was stunned, but also very angry. The more she thought about the billboard, the faster she drove toward Echo Woods. The first thing she was going to do was talk to Sam! All she needed was for people to start asking questions about something she was **not** prepared to discuss! And, after all, it was **her** idea and property!

By the time she neared the exit to Echo Woods, she had decided that she and Sam would be discussing the billboard and few other things as soon as possible.

CHAPTER 24

JUST AS AUDRY TURNED OFF the highway and headed toward home in Echo Woods, she saw flashing red and blue lights in her rearview mirror. Oh, no! What had she done? This was turning into an exasperating day like no other! What now? She slowly pulled to the side of the road, and reached for her wallet to show her driver's license if needed.

As she turned to look out her side window, she saw it was none other than Bow! What was he doing stopping her? Wasn't he in charge of animal control with Loral County?

She lowered her window and saw that he was smiling. He said, "Hey lady, did you know the road is closed up ahead? Didn't you see the detour sign back there?"

"Uh, NO!" she angrily replied. "I guess I didn't. And, am I getting a ticket?"

"No, not this time. I'm just here to serve, ma'am," he said as he gave her a huge grin.

"What on earth is going on to cause a detour?" Audry demanded.

"You didn't know?" Bow asked in surprise. "Well, you should know, because Sam and his people have the road blocked going to your place. They have some large earth-moving machinery that they are slowly moving in there. Since there would be traffic delays, we decided to route a detour around them," Bow explained.

Audry immediately got out of her SUV and shouted. "WE?! Shouldn't I be part of a decision that closes a road to *my* property? That does it! Where is **HE**? I need to talk to him right now!" she demanded.

At that very moment, Audry lost all the composure and restraint she had maintained for far too long.

Bow was not sure how to handle the situation. He had never seen Audry angry, and he certainly had not expected this response from her. She was red-hot mad!

"Uh, well, I don't know, exactly ... but I'm sure there really isn't a problem. He told me that you had some kind of razzle-dazzle new job as special events director for a new St. Louis company and that you would be turning your property into some kind of animal preserve, or something," Bow explained.

"Oh? Did he **really**!" Audry emphatically replied.

"Well, congratulations!" Bow said, and gave her a hearty pat on her back.

"Thank you, I, uh, I think," Audry said as she choked on her words. "But construction?"

"Oh, you know Sam. He is always scheduling and planning stuff," Bow said with a chuckle. "He said he had it on good authority that some of the major earth moving and construction had to happen before the rains start in August. Supposedly, Sam thinks we are going to have an unusually wet summer and he has to get started right away to get things finished by next spring."

"Oh, uh-huh," Audry responded with total confusion written across her face.

Regaining some composure in light of this new information, Audry wondered about exactly where Sam **did** get his information anyway!

"Hey, do you want to grab a cup of coffee at Franco's Café?" Bow asked.

Resigning herself to forces that made no sense, Audry slowly released her anger. After a while, she quietly replied, "Sure, I think I could probably use a cup ... about now."

As they sipped their coffee in the café, Audry asked Bow if there was anything else she had missed in just the short time she had been away from Echo Woods. She thought to herself that Sam and his people certainly did live in another time and dimension, and that made it even more difficult to stay on top of his activities, as if she **ever** could.

Finally, Audry said that she had "heard" about an organization that was interested in developing in the area. She had negotiated with them over the use of her land, too. The group was now looking for somebody to manage the animal preserve operations.

"Actually, I think you would be perfect, Bow. And, since the county doesn't have money to build a new shelter, I think the new preserve would be what you have been wanting to see in Loral County for a long time," Audry said with a very reassuring smile. "Maybe you should contact them."

"You really think so?" Bow asked, surprised.

"Well, maybe this is what you have been waiting for, Bow. I'll try to find their contact information for you, if you're interested, and you can send them your letter of interest," Audry suggested.

After leaving the café, Audry was glad she had seen Bow and had calmed down. She still wanted to talk to Sam and tell him that he had to stop with the sudden surprises! They would have to work *together* on this project!

She drove down the road toward her house but then had to stop. There, in and around the barn and outbuildings, were construction trucks and heavy equipment parked everywhere.

And, no surprise, at the center of a crowd of construction workers was Sam, giving directions and writing on his very small notepad.

Audry needed to clear her head, and she knew the best way for that to happen was to take Maggie for a walk. Together they walked up the pathway to the property near the site of the old fairgrounds. Once there, Audry sat on a large rock and let Maggie explore. Gradually after calming down, she looked out upon the land and imagined what the new fairgrounds would be like—amusement rides, a special arena where animals could be seen, and an adoption center where animals could be placed in forever homes.

As her mind wandered, she envisioned pineapple whip, just like she had when she was little, and wonderful prizes for the largest vegetables grown. Then, Audry's thoughts were interrupted by a very familiar voice. Of course. It was Sam.

"Hi ho. This is going to bring a lot of people and animals a lot of happiness, Audry," Sam said.

"Oh, really? You think so, Sam?" Audry said still somewhat angry with him. "Well, it has not made me happy, Sam that you have moved forward with construction *and* a billboard sign promoting this place without even discussing it with me!"

"I know. It is a lot to take in. You hoopies do move a lot slower than me and my people," Sam softly said. "But our intentions are all the same. And, I apologize for upsetting you. I just had to get things moving because we are going to have a really wet summer, and I know you want everything finished by next spring," Sam explained.

"Yes, Bow told me," Audry replied.

"He did? Well, he's a really good young man, Audry. I was hoping I could show you some of the drawings that you haven't seen yet. Maybe we could do that now?" Sam asked.

"Oh, I suppose so, since, I seem to be the last one to know what's really going on …" Audry said, still annoyed.

As Audry marched back to the house, Maggie scampered and sniffed the ground for scents of rabbits and any other animals that shared the property with her. She ran in large circles and always came back to Sam's side and nuzzled his hand. He then removed a small treat from one of his many pockets, gave it to Maggie and watched her take off again, showing both of them just how fast she could run.

Once back in Audry's kitchen, Sam gently removed the old yellow rolls of sketches from his pack. Carefully, he rolled them out on Audry's table.

"You remember these from the other day, right?" Sam asked.

"Yes, and you said they were used by your people to build the original buildings on the fairgrounds," Audry replied.

"Yes, I did. But, do you know who drew these sketches and the plans?" Sam asked.

"Well, no," Audry replied.

"Look in the lower box on the right side," Sam instructed.

There in the lower right-hand corner of each roll was a date and signature. In elegant, cursive writing was the signature of Jacob Merryweather.

"Oh dear," Audry said in a hushed voice. "That is the signature of my grandpa's great-great grandfather?"

With reverence, Sam replied, "Yes, it most certainly is. Now does all of this make more sense to you, my dear?"

With eyebrows raised, Audry asked in a very sincere and respectful tone, "Did your people know him?"

"Well, you might say that. But I know without a doubt, he would be very proud of you and what you have planned for the Merryweather homestead," Sam said. "Echo Woods is a good place. Remember me telling you how Echo Woods got its name? It was based upon the thought that what you give, you get, and that life is like an echo. What you send out, comes back. Well, it was Jacob Merryweather who said that," Sam quietly explained.

CHAPTER 25

WHILE SAM HAD CONSTRUCTION WELL under way, Audry decided to try and finish some of the projects inside her home. It seemed like it was a never-ending project, because she kept being interrupted with animal relocations and emergencies or trips out of town.

Regardless, she managed to paint the walls downstairs, refinish the woodwork, hang a couple of her mother's paintings, set up her entertainment center, and replace some old furniture. There was one large painting of her mother's she had yet to hang at the end of the hallway upstairs.

Oh, and she still needed to search the attic or a storage closet in the basement for the old family diaries and reference books that used to be on the shelves in her grandpa's library.

But her "to do" list was getting shorter. One of her last big projects was to schedule service with an energy specialist to make the house warmer in winter and cooler in summer. Their service could provide new insulation in her home. The technician, Rick, toured the house, looked in the attic, took many measurements, and scheduled a time with Audry to install new insulation.

Surprisingly, there were no interruptions between the tech's visit and the day he and his helpers arrived with a truckload of batts of carefully measured insulation to install in the attic and recesses of the old house.

Working away in her office as the crew went about their installation, Audry was interrupted by Rick.

"Miss Merryweather, there is something really strange about your house," he began.

"Yes?" she replied.

"Well, we carefully measured the inside of the house, garage, attic and places where we could install insulation," he explained. "But the measurements in the attic do not match up with the measurements in one of your upstairs spare bedrooms."

"Okay, so what does that mean?" she asked.

Rick explained, "The bedroom interior outside of the closet measures 14 feet by 12 feet. The closet is 2 feet deep and 14 feet wide. But the attic above the bedroom measures 22 feet by 14 feet. If you subtract the 2 feet for the closet, that still makes the attic above the bedroom 20 by 14 feet. There is 8 feet by 14 feet of space beyond that closet," He explained as his eyebrows rose.

"Wh-at?" Audry stuttered in surprise. "That makes no sense. Please show me."

Together they walked upstairs to the farthest extra bedroom with a couple of large windows that made you feel like you were part of the large ash trees outside. She remembered when she visited her grandparents as a child that this room was where her grandmother stored boxes of giftwrap. It also held a hall tree with lots of old hats and coats. It was rarely used except for occasional overnight guests.

Aside from that, it now had just a bed and a small dressing table with a large mirror that hung above it.

Rick waved his arm toward the closet and said, "There must be something else behind that closet."

He opened a rather large door and pulled a cord that hung from the ceiling. A single light bulb lit up the interior. The wood floor of the closet was made of cedar and showed little signs of wear. The interior sides of the closet were made of cedar as well, which made it perfect for storing bedding and fine clothes that could be protected from moths that liked to munch on certain fabrics.

Although it **looked** like a normal closet, upon closer inspection, Rick pointed out an unusual feature. There were wooden plugs that appeared at one-foot intervals in a straight line up and down in the left corner. Then, he showed her that 16 inches to the right, the pattern of wooden plugs appeared again. The same plug patterns occurred again at 16-inch intervals. Altogether there were six vertical rows of plugs, stopping approximately at about eight feet to the right.

"I think these are removable, Miss Merryweather, and there is something behind the back of this closet," he shared in a hushed tone.

"Oh, my," Audry responded as she felt her heart racing. "Well, I dunno. Would they be hard to remove?"

"No, as long as you want them removed. I won't charge you for that. Frankly, I've never seen anything like this, and I am just as curious as you. Great carpentry work by the way," Rick admitted.

Audry thought to herself, "Just when things seemed like they could be normal, they aren't."

"Sure, but can the wood be put back?" she asked Rick.

"Oh, you bet. I will just need to get some tools and I'll be right back," he assured her.

It took some time while Rick carefully removed each peg and placed it in a paper bag for replacement later. After the last peg was removed, Rick used a hammer and screwdriver to tap and remove the wooden panel at its seams in the ceiling and along the sides. Slowly, he gently pulled and tugged until the panel fell forward and a sudden gush of air rushed out.

Audry jumped from the sound of the air, and released a bit of anxiety that had built up within her.

Rick maneuvered the panel and slid it to reveal an opening beyond the old building studs. He then flicked on a bright flashlight and motioned for Audry to look into the area that had been hidden by the closet.

Audry's eyes grew wide and she gasped as she first saw built-in shelves with too many very old books to count. The lighting was very poor, and she asked Rick if it was safe to step inside the area.

"Sure. Here, use my flashlight," he said as he handed it to her.

Timidly, Audry entered the space that had not seen light in a very long time. She searched the room briefly with the flashlight and saw a cord hanging from the ceiling attached to a socket holding a single light bulb. She gingerly crept to the cord and tugged at its knot on the end. Amazingly, the light came on.

Astonished, she was overcome by memories. There was a small simple wooden table to the side. On top sat the Civil War bucket that her father and Uncle Mike had discovered in the old persimmon grove. On a shelf on the side wall next to it were the items that had once been concealed in the bucket. Professionally displayed inside a glass-covered case were the five coins, the straight edge razor and the slave tag along with a formal printed description. The items looked as they had when she last saw them as a seven-year-old girl.

"Oh, dear," Audry muttered and slightly gasped.

Rick asked, "You okay?"

"Yes, I'm fine actually. These are family heirlooms, some I've seen and some I can't even imagine. I'll meet you downstairs later, if you don't mind," she responded.

Taking the cue that she wanted to be left alone, Rick left, and Audry slowly turned her attention back to the contents of the room.

Along one wall was an antique trunk. Next to it stood a very sturdy cabinet with many shelves. Upon closer inspection she saw the lower half contained large shelves that held many crocks of all sizes. Lying on a shorter shelf above the crocks were all types of wooden tools—spoons, small scoops and other curious pieces. Alongside the wooden tools were several mortar and pestle sets. Then the rows of shelves that rose to the top of the cabinet contained all sizes and shapes of glass bottles—some were elegant but most of them were simply round or square. Most were dark brown glass with stoppers. Each had a paper label with barely visible ink that had long faded with time.

Lined up along the wall that had once served as the back of the closet were three wooden chairs. Next to them in one corner, Audry saw sturdy shelves mounted on the wall that rose about five feet tall. Lining the shelves was antique equipment—two tripods, several old cameras, and a brass surveyor's sextant.

Audry couldn't contain her curiosity and moved over to the old trunk. Surprisingly, it did not have a lock, and the lid opened with little effort. Inside its musty contents, she found two dark heavy comforters and several gray woolen blankets.

As she continued to try to make sense of everything in this hidden room, she spied a cluster of framed pictures on shelves along the farthest wall. Looking closer, she saw pictures of her dad and Uncle Mike as children and many pictures of other very old people she did not recognize. Alone next to the pictures was a fragile, leather-bound book with gold lettering that read "Journal."

Her attention then turned to a framed hand-drawn map that hung on the wall next to the framed pictures. Although its glass covering was dusty and cloudy from age and the map's ink was faded, Audry could clearly see from its outline that it was the state of Missouri and small areas of each of its surrounding states. There were lines drawn along the eastern and western edges of the state that ended in Kansas and Illinois. Along these lines and at some locations in between there were X marks. This indeed was a curious depiction of Missouri. She had a feeling it too was connected to the Civil War era, just like the old bucket. She'd have to follow up with a trip back to the old history museum in St. Louis sometime and find out.

Finally, as she finished surveying the room, her gaze stopped at the top shelf of a small cabinet. There stationed proudly in a single wooden base was an antique tintype. Only then did things begin to fall into place. Imprinted in the tin were images of "little people" standing in front of a large sign that read, "Echo Woods."

Audry couldn't wait to spend more time in this room. It would be like taking a journey back in time and discovering the answers to a number of her lifelong questions. However, she had other important things that needed her attention at the moment.

Her thoughts raced with excitement. Maybe in the future she would merge this room with the bedroom and call it her Merryweather legacy room. Regardless, it would be the most special room in her home.

CHAPTER 26

ABOUT NINE MONTHS AFTER SAM had shown Jacob Merryweather's sketches to Audry, the Loral County Preserve and Fairgrounds was finally open to the public. Yes, Sam had been correct about the unusual rainy summer, and with his advice the preserve and fairgrounds opened in spring, right on schedule.

After that, throngs of people visited the preserve during Showcase Day once a week. That was when Jacy's group of students would lead the latest "residents" into the special arena where they could be viewed by qualified potential adopters. Because of the public relations campaigns that Audry had created, every animal had its portrait posted on a special website that could be seen worldwide. Regardless of its status, every animal was provided a safe haven and care that few facilities across the country could match. Of course, Stella, Sunny, and a few other early residents remained permanently at the preserve. Stella became the official mascot because of her being a Missouri mule like no other.

Oh, yes, the population of rescue animals did increase! Significantly! Once the word got around, the local population became very mindful about stray animals across Loral County and stepped up to make sure they were directed to the new preserve for proper care. There were plenty of accommodations, and the animals were carefully supervised and managed by Bow. He had also played a key role in creating a satellite veterinary hospital that was staffed by selected students from the university's veterinary school. The hospital gave the animals the opportunity to live in a humane environment, free from abuse and with plenty of quality care. And, most of all, they got plenty of food.

Simple healthcare needs of the animals were performed by the students of the satellite vet school. This resulted in a greater interest in science among Jacy's kids, and their teachers saw an improvement in their science grades in school.

With the increase in the animal population at the preserve, the responsibilities also grew for the River City kids. They learned how to care for the animals in new ways. They also played key roles in a new alternative visitation program set up by Jacy. This program provided the opportunity for the kids to take dogs for visits to residents of nursing homes or people who were housebound. The kids named the program, "Dog Days." Not only did the program benefit the clients who sometimes rarely had visitors, it also gave the children the opportunity to learn about their elders and listen to some amazing stories.

Because of Sam's smart ideas about energy, the preserve and fairgrounds were mostly powered by renewable energy, and recycling was strongly supported. And as could be expected, he continued to provide Audry with ideas for improvements. She didn't always agree, but she finally decided Sam's ideas usually were successful. She also knew that protest was just a waste of her energy.

The new fairgrounds never failed to attract large crowds. It immediately became a top tourist destination for summer family entertainment throughout the Midwest. There were cornfields transformed into a maze, the carnival rides, the petting zoo, and the Seven Sisters Smorgy that never ceased to get rave reviews. Evening concerts and performances under the stars in the community center provided a stellar evening for all who attended.

Bow worked hard and took a lot of pride in managing the animals and adoptions. But he also made sure that the grounds were clean and that guests were safe. He and Audry worked together very well, and as time permitted, they went to Springfield for a change of scenery and always dinner at Nico's. But foremost, they were always brainstorming about ways to improve and expand the preserve and fairgrounds.

By the end of its first summer, the first county fair awarded prizes for the top entries in crafts, homegrown vegetables and fruits, and homemade preserves and canned goods. Along with the award of prizes, a ribbon-cutting ceremony took place to celebrate the official grand opening. Invitations were sent out to the Missouri governor, elected officials, Humane Society members, animal lovers, and special guests far and wide.

The preparation for this immense event consumed many hours of Audry's time. The categories for prizes ranged from the biggest watermelon to the best crafted quilt, and all the "BEST of the BEST" homegrown and homemade items in between.

The carnival had brought in its newest and most exciting rides. The stage was prepared for the prize-winning awards, and a podium and sound system were set up for the governor to give a brief speech.

On the day of the ribbon-cutting ceremony, Bow brought in some technical workers to test the equipment, including the gigantic Ferris wheel.

Finally, at sundown, the festivities began. Before the crowds could enter the fairground, the governor addressed the residents of Loral County and praised the work of all who helped to make the Loral County Preserve and Fairgrounds the best new humane enterprise not only in Missouri but also in the Midwest. At last, the mayor of Echo Woods flipped on the lights to the fairgrounds and cut the ribbon allowing families to shop, eat, and enjoy the thrills of the carnival rides.

Audry was overjoyed with the success of the evening and grateful to now see the preserve become a reality. As the evening got underway, she noticed that Nico and Maria had arrived. She walked over to them, and both Nico and Maria hugged her and congratulated her on the success of the evening.

Satisfied that the rest of the evening would take care of itself, Audry gathered her bags and started walking back to her house. Suddenly, the Ferris wheel music stopped and this was followed by the sound of Nico's booming voice making an announcement over the sound system.

"Ladies and gentlemen. May I have your attention, please? It seems that the Ferris wheel has amazingly stopped, and I would like to draw your attention to a man at the top who has a special message."

Audry was stricken with terror. She asked herself, "How could a well-planned evening go so haywire?!?!" She turned and rushed back to the main area. The crowd had grown quiet and a spotlight was now shining at the top of the Ferris wheel. She was very confused and moved quickly toward Nico.

Alarmed, she breathlessly asked Nico, "What on earth is going on?!"

"Well, look at the top of the Ferris wheel, Audry," he replied with a huge grin.

Shading her eyes from the flashback of the glaring light, she saw Bow at the very top of the Ferris wheel, holding a huge sign. Squinting to read the sign, she almost fainted as she read, **"AUDRY, WILL YOU MARRY ME?"**

At Nico's direction, the music resumed, the Ferris wheel continued to turn, and Bow rode to the ground. There he got off, walked to Audry and took her hand. Audry smiled and hugged him. A small crowd hidden behind the carnival trucks cheered and whistled. This was followed by applause, whoops, whistles, and hollers by the huge fairground crowd.

Audry looked at Bow, Nico, and Maria, and knew that they, as well as Sam and his people were her new family, even though some of them would never be visible to the common population.

HYPERLINK RESOURCES

CHAPTER 1
Ozarks (Encyclopedia Britannica)
https://www.britannica.com/place/Ozark-Mountains

CHAPTER 4
Mississippi River (Encyclopedia Britannica)
www.britannica.com/place/Mississippi-River

Barge (Wikipedia)
https://en.wikipedia.org/wiki/Barge

St. Louis World's Fair (St. Louis, MO, Government)
https://www.stlouis-mo.gov/archive/history-forest-park/fair.html

Louisiana Purchase (Encyclopedia Britannica)
https://www.britannica.com/event/Louisiana-Purchase

Underground Railroad (Ducksters Education Site)
http://www.ducksters.com/history/civil war/underground railroad.php

Missouri in the Civil War (Wikipedia)
https://en.wikipedia.org/wiki/
Missouri in the American Civil War

CHAPTER 6
Missouri Mules (State Symbols USA)
https://statesymbolsusa.org/symbol-official-item/missouri/state-horse/missouri-mule

Purple Martins (Audubon Field Guide)
http://www.audubon.org/field-guide/bird/purple-martin

Branson (Official Branson Website)
www.branson.com

CHAPTER 7
Marker Trees (Wikipedia)
https://en.wikipedia.org/wiki/Trail_trees

Red-Tailed Hawk (National Geographic)
www.nationalgeographic.com/animals/birds/r/red-tailed-hawk/

Missouri (Wikipedia)
https://en.wikipedia.org/wiki/Missouri

Pony Express (Wikipedia)
https://en.wikipedia.org/wiki/Pony_Express

Cherokee (Cherokee Nation)
www.cherokee.org/About-The-Nation/History/Facts/Our-History

Trail of Tears (Cherokee National Cultural Resource Center)
http://www.cherokee.org/About-The-Nation/History/Trail-of-Tears/A-Brief-History-of-the-Trail-of-Tears

Katy Trail State Park (MO State Parks)
https://mostateparks.com/park/katy-trail-state-park

CHAPTER 8
Monarch Butterflies (National Geographic)
http://www.nationalgeographic.com/animals/invertebrates/m/monarch-butterfly/

CHAPTER 11
Zink (Iowa State University)
www.music.iastate.edu/antiqua/zink.htm

CHAPTER 15
Acifidity Bag (Wikipedia)
https://en.wikipedia.org/wiki/Asafoetida

CHAPTER 18
St. Charles, Missouri (City of St. Charles)
www.stcharlescitymo.gov

St. Louis Art Museum (St. Louis Art Museum)
www.slam.org

CHAPTER 19
Land Mobile Radio [LMR] (Wikipedia)
https://en.wikipedia.org/wiki/
Land_mobile_radio_system

CHAPTER 25
Tintype (Wikipedia)
https://en.wikipedia.org/wiki/Tintype

ADDITIONAL RESOURCES

Civil War on the Western Border (The Kansas City Public Library)
Includes Lesson Plans – Grade Levels 8 - 12
http://www.civilwaronthewesternborder.org/
encyclopedia/underground-railroad

ARTISTS' BIOGRAPHIES

Barbara Peck, PhD

A Missouri native and lifelong resident, Dr. Barbara Peck earned her PhD in Art Education at the University of Missouri in Columbia.

Her artwork in the book include the illustrations of the gravedigger's cottage, the Merryweather barn and homestead, Stella the mule, Maggie the dog, and Civil War treasures found on the Merryweather property.

An educator for some 30 years, she has taught a broad scope of students at both high school and college levels.

Her love of art is surpassed only by her love of travel and spending time with her family.

She freely shares her personal philosophy of art and says: "Learning to draw is like learning a language. And, its value comes when you have something to say."

Dr. Peck may be contacted at: bpeck101@gmail.com

David Diekamp

The five main characters in the book (Audry, Sam, Bow, Jacy, and Django) were drawn by professional designer and illustrator, David Diekamp. A Missouri native, David earned a bachelor's degree from College of the Ozarks where he studied graphic design.

He began his career with the University of Missouri's College of Agriculture, where he designed publications and display materials. Later, David discovered a colored pencil technique that led to new illustration opportunities as a freelance artist.

As his clientele has increased via word-of-mouth, David has accumulated a significant portfolio of diverse illustrations. He has pursued a direction of realism in his work through which he has successfully reproduced complex textures, patterns and intricate details. David's greatest satisfaction comes from the look of appreciation from his clients regardless of the challenges.

David resides in Macon, Missouri, with his wife Jennifer, and their three children Jake, Luke, and Katie.

To view David's portfolio, please visit this online address:
https://www.behance.net/DDIEKAMP4439

To discuss projects and fee schedules, contact David at:
diekampillutrations@gmail.com

ABOUT THE AUTHOR

Born and raised in Missouri, the author spent most of her adult life in Nevada and California. She earned a B.A. degree in communications at the University of Nevada—Las Vegas (UNLV). Contact her via email at: LuckyMaxwill@gmail.com

Printed in the United States
By Bookmasters